Business Writing for Innovators and Change-Makers

Business Writing for Innovators and Change-Makers

Dawn Henwood

BEP BUSINESS EXPERT PRESS

First published in 2020 by
Business Expert Press, LLC
222 East 46th Street, New York, NY 10017
www.businessexpertpress.com

ISBN-13: 978-1-95152-778-5 (paperback)
ISBN-13: 978-1-95152-779-2 (e-book)

Business Expert Press Corporate Communication Collection

Collection ISSN: 2156-8162 (print)
Collection ISSN: 2156-8170 (electronic)

Cover image licensed by Ingram Image, StockPhotoSecrets.com
Cover and interior design by S4Carlisle Publishing Services Private Ltd., Chennai, India

First edition: 2020

10 9 8 7 6 5 4 3 2 1

Printed in the United States of America.

Dedication

For my daughter Claire, who is my Sunshine.

Abstract

Business Writing for Innovators and Change-Makers is a writing guidebook with street-smarts. It recognizes the unique communication challenges entrepreneurs face and offers clear action steps for tackling them.

As an entrepreneur with a pioneering product or service to offer the world, you can't rely on templates to get your meaning across. You need a set of writing strategies that are quick to implement and easy to adapt to a variety of communication situations, from e-mails to pitch decks.

Dawn Henwood provides a simple, flexible approach to writing that will open your eyes to the subtle ways written communication can engage and motivate your target audience. Each short chapter includes:

- Advice from an innovative entrepreneur
- Concise, practical tips you can put to use right away
- Insights to help you become more productive and persuasive
- Checklist to help you coach yourself and your team to better writing

Whether you are just starting your business or scaling up to the next level of success, you'll find Dawn's straightforward teaching just the help you need to make your message heard. This book will empower you to build your confidence as a communicator, strengthen your brand, and increase the impact you have on customers and clients.

Keywords

marketing; marketing collateral; messaging; pitch decks; pitching; proposals; technical writing; grant applications; business plans; business writing; business communication; e-mail; productivity; blogging

Contents

Preface

As an entrepreneur, you're continually pushing yourself beyond your comfort zone. Blazing your own trail requires you to learn new skills and pick up tools you haven't handled before or perhaps have even intentionally avoided. I'm not a "numbers person," but running my own consulting business has forced me to learn to navigate spreadsheets and financial statements. Likewise, I'd rather get my teeth drilled than make a prospecting phone call, but—to my great amazement—I've learned how to do that too.

I'm amazed every time I pick up the phone to approach a potential client because I used to suffer from what I called a profound phone allergy. I dreaded not just making calls but taking them too. Even the thought of dialing a colleague or client I knew well would start my heart pitter-pattering and make my gut churn.

Then I met Mary Jane Copps, aka The Phone Lady (www.thephonelady.com), who introduced me to a step-by-step process for starting a phone conversation. I came to realize that the ability to build relationships over the phone isn't an innate talent but a learnable skill set. I'd misdiagnosed myself as having a constitutional deficiency, an "allergy," when I only lacked knowledge and practice.

In my 20 years as a writing instructor and coach, most of the people I've trained have held a similarly mistaken belief about their writing abilities. They've bought into the popular assumption that strong writers are born, not made. And they've been startled to discover how much more fluent and effective their written communication becomes as soon as they stop viewing writing as a gift and start seeing it as group of techniques that anyone can master.

As an entrepreneur leading an innovative business or social enterprise, you need a particularly adaptable set of writing skills that will enable you to tackle each new communication challenge as it arises. In a large, established organization, people produce a limited range of documents, determined by their role. Junior engineers produce incident reports, while senior engineers write technical reports and contribute to proposals. Marketers produce marketing collateral, accountants report on financial matters, and learning specialists develop training materials. But as an innovator at the helm of an evolving organization, you're called upon to create (or supervise the creation of) a wide variety of writing that spans multiple business functions.

This week, the challenge might be to write a critical e-mail following up with a prospective client you met at a networking event. Next week, you might be faced with drafting a proposal, revising your web copy, or starting your first white paper. Or you might find yourself Googling to clarify the kind of document a client is expecting, especially if they've thrown an acronym or a piece of jargon at you, such as SOW (Statement of Work), pitch deck, or TOR (Terms of Reference document). As you know, when you head into the wilds of entrepreneurship, no one gives you a map of the territory. Nor do you get a guidebook to all the different kinds of writing you'll need to produce.

This book doesn't pretend to provide a comprehensive guidebook to entrepreneurial communication—because no book could possibly cover all the peculiar writing tasks you'll encounter along your entrepreneurial journey. Instead, it gives you practical tips and tools for producing the kinds of writing that power up innovative organizations. These are the types, or *genres*, of writing that fuel growth. They attract clients and customers, secure capital, and engage your client base in an ongoing conversation centered on your organization's values and mission.

Think of this book as a writing coach rather than as a writing instructor. I suggest that you start with the first chapter, which outlines an agile writing process you can apply to any kind of business writing. I've dubbed this method the Change-Maker Writing Process because it addresses the special challenges you face when you're communicating at the edge of innovation. Writing persuasively about a brand new solution, or a solution your readers don't grasp from a technical perspective, requires you to pay particular attention to what your audience *does* understand and value so you can connect with them in ways that go beyond the cognitive.

Once you've learned the Change-Maker Writing Process, I invite you to explore the other chapters in whatever order makes sense to you, perhaps on an as-needed basis. You'll find that each chapter contains straightforward tips, examples, and models you can apply on the spot, along with a handy checklist.

Throughout the book, you'll also meet other innovators who have shared with me their insights into producing powerful writing that drives business results. Like my favorite writing guru Peter Elbow, I believe firmly that "everyone can write,"[1] and the real entrepreneurs featured in this book show how true that is. None of them are "trained" or "professional" writers, yet they're all using writing to connect with their target audiences and move their businesses forward. I'm grateful to all of these folks for giving us glimpses into their personal writing process, and I hope you find their stories relevant and motivational.

A wise colleague once told me, "You never finish a piece of writing; you just abandon it." In abandoning this book, I'm conscious that it could be improved in many places. I'd welcome any feedback you have for bettering the next edition. Feel free to send me an e-mail (dawn@dawnhenwood.com), or connect with me on LinkedIn.

Best wishes as you set out to take your writing, and your business, to the next level!

Dawn

---

[1] Although Peter Elbow has published many scholarly books and articles on writing, his work is very accessible. For practical tips to make writing easier, check out his collection of essays called *Everyone Can Write* (New York, NY: Oxford University Press, 2000).

Acknowledgments

No writer is an island, and this book exists only thanks to the goodwill of many busy entrepreneurs who generously shared their insights into the real-world challenges of communicating at the edge of innovation. I'm grateful to all the people who agreed to my request for an interview: Mike Cyr, Anirudh Kuhl, Antoine Bonicalzi, Christine Ward-Paige, Hussein Hallak, Mandy Wintink, Janet Bannister, Kevin Canning, Kyle Rogers, Richard Howe, Laurie Sinclair, Karen Lightstone, Stephen Bartol, Valerie Song, Kelsey Snowdon, and Dave Belt. I learned much from each of you and treasure the different ways you helped bring the book's concepts to life.

I'm also grateful for Jennifer LaPlante and Peter Secord, who gave me valuable feedback on the draft manuscript. Your interest in the project kept me charging for the finish line, and your insights have improved the final product.

Thank you to the staff at BEP who made the messy work of birthing a book a seamless process, especially Rob Zwettler, Debbie DuFrene, Charlene Kronstedt, and Rene Caroline.

And many thanks to my partner Jack Kivik for helping with the tedious process of combing through the manuscript for typos and punctuation errors.

Finally, I'm especially thankful for my daughter, Claire, who never once complained that book-writing cut into our summer vacation time and cheered me on from chapter to chapter. She inspires me daily in more ways than I can count.

CHAPTER 1

The Change-Maker Writing Process

If you want to improve *what* you write, you need to start by improving *how* you write. In this section, you'll throw away any "rules" you've heard about writing and instead embrace a user-centered approach you can adapt to each communication situation you face.

Before we dive in, take a moment to notice three key terms in the above paragraph:

- **User-centered**—As cognitive scientist Mike Sharples showed way back before "design thinking" became trendy,[1] writing is essentially a design process. It starts not with a vision of the final product but with a deep understanding of the user's/audience's perspective and needs.
- **Adapt**—While the Change-Maker Writing Process provides guidelines for you to follow, you'll need to flex those to fit the kind of document you're writing and its context, including the amount of time you have to spend writing.
- **Communication situation**—The process you're about to learn will help you communicate more effectively in face-to-face interactions as well as on the page or screen. You can use the Change-Maker Writing Process to create presentations, conduct client meetings, and even use the phone more effectively.

Ready to roll up your sleeves and get started? I suggest you read this chapter with a pen and paper handy so you can take notes and brainstorm about how you could apply the Change-Maker guidelines to a real communication situation you're facing (or have faced) this week.

---

[1]M. Sharples. 1999. *How We Write: Writing as Creative Design* (London, UK: Routledge).

Key Principles for Producing Change-Maker Writing

Change-Maker writing moves people. It may also educate them along the way, but its ultimate goal is persuasive. It aims to get people to join your mission and buy into your new, creative solution to a challenging problem.

If Change-Maker writing simply teaches people about your products or explains how they work, it has missed the mark. You don't want well-educated customers. You want buying customers.

The same applies to investors. Yes, it's critical that a potential investor understand all the inner workings of your product, but unless you're also hoping to bring the investor on board as your new chief engineer, that's not what really matters. Persuasion, not technical proficiency, is what will put funds in your bank account.

To convince people to buy your ideas and your offerings, you need a writing process that centers on your audience, their problems, and targeted solutions to those problems. You also need a process that's streamlined and quick because "writer" is just one of the many job titles you fill on any given day. In other words, the way you produce writing should be as nimble and flexible as you and your organization are.

Two key principles will help you develop a writing process you can adapt to the many different communication challenges you encounter. The first of these principles is *creative destruction*. Throw away all the "rules" you've learned about writing, and tune out the mental chatter that tells you what "good" writers do and don't do. Instead, start thinking about writing as a series of interrelated activities that anyone can master with guidance and practice. If you can learn to ride a bike or code an app or cook an omelet, then you can certainly learn the craft of written communication.

The second principle for writing success is *design thinking*. Designers create artifacts that solve problems, and so do writers.

Just take a look around your home or office. From pens to pots, door handles to dog food dispenser, every item you see was created to solve a problem. For instance, my favorite pens have a cushiony rubber grip to solve the problem of hand fatigue. My double-handled pots solve the problem of imbalanced cooking utensils and long handles crowding the stovetop. My super-light Mac Air solves the problem of having to lug around a heavy laptop.

Take a moment now to scan your environment and consider how the items in it solve problems for you. And now let's consider an everyday example of writing as problem-solving.

Imagine a client sends you a casual e-mail asking to increase the amount of technical support included with the software installation you're doing. That's a problem because your contract with the client doesn't include any tech support. Therefore, the e-mail you design in response to the request has to solve several issues. It must clarify contract terms, ensure that you get paid for all the work you do, satisfy the client, and preserve the positive relationship you have with them.

You can see the potential for conflict among these goals. What makes you happy may not make the client happy. For starters, if you uphold the terms of the contact, you could alienate the client. On the other hand, if you offer free technical support, you'll take a financial loss. In such a situation, the e-mail you write must be a complex and customized solution, carefully crafted to address a multidimensional problem.

This is not the same as saying that the e-mail must *present* a complex solution. The most persuasive solutions are always simple, and in this case, the more straightforward you can make matters for your client, the better. (They're currently confused about the terms of the contract, so your task is to clear up that confusion.)

The e-mail must itself *be* a complex solution. Thinking of a piece of writing as a designed solution means distinguishing between the message the client hears and the process that goes into creating the message. This is exactly what we do with complex technology solutions. For example, when I get in my car to go visit a client, I click on an app that automatically tracks my mileage and calculates the amount to deduct from my taxes. From my perspective, this is a brilliantly simple solution to the problem of recording my travel expenses. But from the perspective of those who created the app, the solution is an astoundingly complex product that involved thousands of hours of coding, raising capital, testing, and marketing.

When you start recognizing writing as the process of designing complex solutions to multifaceted problems, it's easy to see why templates and lists of writing rules offer little help. Such pre-fab solutions fail to take into account the human factors that can complicate business interactions. And there are always human factors.

Human-centered design thinking provides a better way. Designers approach a problem with curiosity, not a pre-formed answer. They start by focusing first on the user of the product or service they're designing. They explore the problem in depth, from the user's perspective, finding out as much as they can about the user's world, their tasks, and their purposes. During this process, they make it a habit to continually second-guess themselves, questioning their own assumptions about what will or won't make a solution effective for the user. Only after they've viewed the problem from the user's point of view do designers articulate the criteria a solution must meet and create a prototype that fits those criteria. After they've built their prototype, they test it out with real users so they can confirm that the item or process they've built works in the real world.

You can follow a similar process to create writing that really works, that communicates clearly with your target audience in ways that build strong business relationships. While such a process may appear laborious, with practice you'll soon find that the steps become intuitive, making your writing both easier to produce and more impactful.

Put Your Audience First

Imagine you're a biomedical engineer who's been asked to design a new device that will allow surgeons to close incisions without sutures or staples. But you've never been in an operating room. Nor have you watched a video of a surgical incision being closed or interviewed a surgeon. Where do you begin?

Without the opportunity to view the end user (the surgeon) in their context, you risk making some serious, even potentially life-threatening, assumptions. You might assume that certain chemical materials would work well, not realizing the way they could interact with the presence of anesthetic in the patient's body. Or you might assume that a device of a certain shape would work, not realizing it wouldn't fit in the tray used to sterilize surgical instruments. Without in-depth knowledge of the user and the user's context, how can you possibly create a viable solution?

If you dive into writing without taking the time to learn about the people who will be reading your words, your solutions (your messages and documents) inevitably flop. Your e-mails go unanswered, your proposals fall flat, and your marketing copy fails to magnetize opportunities. You may be communicating accurately, even clearly, but if you're not connecting with your audience in ways that resonate with them, you're just wasting your time and energy.

But here's the good news: when you invest time in analyzing your audience, you gain instant focus and insight into how to attract and persuade your target readers. And you don't need to hire a research assistant or private eye to investigate your audience. You can collect rich information about your audience by considering four simple questions:

- What is my audience's level of technical *knowledge* about my subject?
- What *fears* keep my audience up at night?
- What *aspirations* does my audience have?
- What *values* does my audience treasure?

The chart below suggests further questions you can ask yourself as you explore each of these aspects of audience analysis (Table 1.1):

Table 1.1 Audience analysis questions

Knowledge	Fears	Aspirations	Values
—What is the audience's level of technical knowledge with regard to the specific subject at hand? —How much history of the subject does the audience have? —What's the audience's interest in acquiring technical knowledge about the subject? —What's the audience's aptitude for acquiring technical knowledge about the subject?	—What problems or worries are keeping the audience up at night? —What "political" issues are causing the audience angst? —What trends in the industry or market are causing concern? —What recognized weaknesses are causing feelings of insecurity? —What past experiences make the audience wary of change? —What makes it hard for the audience to trust you and your company?	—What business goals does the audience want to achieve? —How is the audience's industry and market evolving? —What personal goals do they want to accomplish? —How does the audience like to see themselves?	—What is the audience's sense of purpose (personal and organizational)? —What are the principles the audience won't compromise on? —What qualities does the audience value in a partner? —What qualities does the audience value in communication?

An Example of Audience Analysis in Action

Let's see how these questions help with a specific writing challenge. Imagine you're writing a proposal to introduce a new skin test for multiple sclerosis (MS) into a large hospital. Since nurses would administer the test, you know that the hospital's chief nursing officer Angelica Francis (AF) will be a key reader and decision maker. You've not met Angelica, so you don't have any first-hand knowledge to draw on. Consequently, you mine every information source you can think of to learn as much as you can about her. You consult LinkedIn, Angelica's publications in nursing journals, news stories on the hospital website, and one of Angelica's former staff members, whom you've gotten to know at the gym. Based on this research, you make some inferences about Angelica's knowledge, fears, aspirations, and values, captured in Table 1.2.

With these inferences in hand, you're now well-positioned to craft a proposal that doesn't just provide information but also connects with your target audience emotionally. As you write, you'll keep at the front of your mind the matters Angelica cares most about, and that awareness will guide your creative process. In other words, you'll be able to design a document custom-built for your particular user.

If you've ever helped develop a product or service, then you know that the design process happens as a series of decisions. Writing evolves the same way. Once you've completed your audience analysis, you face decisions in four key areas: content, structure, style, and word choice.

Table 1.3 lists specific design questions you can ask as you start to build your prototype, your draft document. As you read through the questions, apply them to a current writing situation you're facing. You may want to take notes you can refer to later as you start to draft the writing solution for that situation.

Note that I said you'd be able to answer "some" of these questions. In some cases, especially if you've interacted with your reader in person, you'll be able to respond confidently to most of them. In other cases, you may find you can answer only one or two questions per category. That's fine. A little information gives you more persuasive power than no information.

Table 1.2 Audience analysis in action

Knowledge	Fears	Aspirations	Values
—What is the audience's level of technical knowledge with regard to the specific subject at hand? *High. One of the nurses under AF led a recent clinical study of a skin test for lupus.* —How much history of the subject does the audience have? *A moderate amount. AF has been with the hospital only six months, and we've been in discussions with them for two years.* —What's the audience's interest in acquiring technical knowledge about the subject? *High. In the web story announcing AF's new role with the hospital, she's quoted as saying how important it is for practitioners to keep up to date with the latest technological advancements.* —What's the audience's aptitude for acquiring technical knowledge about the subject? *High. AF has a master's degree in science as well as a master's in nursing.*	—What problems or worries are keeping the audience up at night? *Lack of staff. Overworked, stressed-out nurses.* —What "political" issues are causing the audience angst? *Different divisions of the hospital are constantly battling for funding. AF is the only woman on the hospital's executive team.* —What past experiences make the audience wary of change? *AF is a change-maker. She's introduced major changes in every role she's taken on. She may, however, be wary of making a major change just a short time after starting in her new job.* —What makes it hard for the audience to trust you and your company? *We've not yet met in person. We don't have any former practitioners on our team, and we can't offer any clinical evidence yet showing how well the test works.*	—What business goals does the audience want to achieve? *Greater efficiency and better patient care.* —What personal goals do they want to accomplish? *Earn goodwill of her staff by making their job easier. Make her mark in a new organization and role.* —How does the audience like to see themselves? *As a leader. AF's LinkedIn profile uses the words "caring" and "accountable."*	—What is the audience's sense of purpose (personal and organizational)? *The hospital has said it wants to become a leader in alternative, noninvasive testing of chronic disease.* —What are the principles the audience won't compromise on? *More information needed. Best guess: patient safety and quality of care.* —What qualities does the audience value in a partner? *Hard to say, without having met AF.* —What qualities does the audience value in communication? *Both AF's LinkedIn profile and her articles are written in a simple, direct, down-to-earth style.*

Table 1.3 Change-Maker writing design questions

Content	• What topics does my audience care about the most? • What aspects of the product or service I'm describing does my audience care about the most? • What does my audience care about the least? • What does my audience *not* care about at all? • What topics are likely to irritate my audience? • What topics might distract my audience from what I think is important?
Structure	• What content will my audience want to access right away? • What's the minimum amount of context my audience needs to understand and accept what I have to say? • What does my audience need to understand about the purpose of the document? • What headings will make it easy for my audience to preview and navigate the document? • What (if any) content will my audience appreciate in an appendix rather than in the main document?
Style	• What's the relationship between my audience and me? • What level of politeness does the relationship warrant? • What level of formality will the audience appreciate? • What style qualities will appeal to the audience (e.g., positivity, brevity, directness, accuracy)?
Word choice	• What specialized technical terms are familiar to my audience? • What jargon or shop-talk is familiar to the audience? • What favorite words or phrases does the audience have? • What "hot-button" words or phrases might trigger a negative knee-jerk reaction from the audience?

A word of caution as you start to get into the habit of analyzing your audiences in depth: regardless of how much audience "data" you collect, bear in mind that none of it is "hard data." Be careful that your inferences don't lead you to indulge in mistaken assumptions or stereotyping or to jump to unfounded conclusions. Designers continually query their assumptions, and so should you.

In fact, you should look for opportunities to test your assumptions. For instance, in the hospital example, if you haven't yet met with the primary decision maker who will be reading your proposal, you might be able to arrange a meeting before you start writing. If you're responding to an RFP (Request for Proposals), then you may find yourself up against a rigid submission process that prevents you from approaching Angelica directly. But if the situation is less formal, then you could perhaps set up a quick chat to clarify what Angelica expects from the proposal. As any designer will tell you, whenever you can involve the user in the design process, you greatly increase your chances of creating something the user actually wants to engage with.

What about Writing for Multiple Readers?

In the perfect world, you know the people who will be reading your document, and you're able to research them thoroughly. But in the real world, you're often creating documents that will be read by multiple people, some of whom may be unknown to you. How can you analyze an audience that is invisible to you?

You broaden your analysis so you can investigate readers not by name but by the community or professional group to which they belong. In the case of the hospital proposal, you'll want to start by considering who the gatekeeper audience might be. Who will receive the document and decide whether or not it makes it to Angelica's desk? Then, you'll also want to consider other readers with whom Angelica will share the document. This secondary audience could include members of the hospital executive team, staff members who would be involved in implementing the skin test, and perhaps also a hospital doctor who conducts research on MS.

Through some Web sleuthing, we might be able to identify some of these possible other readers by name and conduct research on them, the same way we investigated Angelica. We would then look for common ground among the different readers and tailor our proposal so it appeals to shared interests and values (keeping in mind that Angelica is the primary decision maker and that persuading her remains our primary concern).

But let's say we can't identify our "other" readers individually. We still have leads to follow because we can consider each reader in terms of their group identity. For instance, we may not be able to point to the hospital executives by name, but we can do some research into the typical professional background, job responsibilities, and concerns of senior hospital administrators. (This is where trade journals, blogs, and websites of professional associations become very useful.) We can do the same with nurses who specialize in working with MS patients and with medical researchers.

Yes, this is painstaking work, but it pays huge dividends in terms of the way readers react to your writing. A generic document written for no particular audience comes across as impersonal ("Just another technical proposal—*yawn*…"), while a document tailored to the specific audience makes readers sit up and take notice ("Wow! These folks really get who we are and what we're trying to achieve").

Gaining Efficiency

Right about now, you may be wondering just how on earth you're going to find time to analyze your readers in such depth when writing tasks are already stealing more than their share of the day. The key is to give your method for producing writing an Agile upgrade. Three helpful concepts will enable you to do that: process, proportion, and prototyping.

1. **Embrace audience analysis as a *process*** that will quickly become a habit. As you internalize the process, you'll soon become more efficient at it. By training your curiosity, you'll develop a kind of writer's intuition.

   As you become more used to investigating your audience, you'll also tweak the analytical process to suit your needs. As you experiment with the charts in this chapter, I'd encourage you to develop your own questions, checklists, and resource lists to help you quickly drill down into deep audience insights.

2. **Redistribute the *proportion* of time you spend in writing production.** Much of the activity of writing, including audience analysis, occurs off-page as the writer wrestles internally with such matters as design, organization, and tone. Yet many writers allocate most of their writing time to production, the external act of forming words and sentences. In fact, this aspect of writing should suck up only about a third of your total writing time.

   Challenge yourself to become more efficient at production so you have ample time to invest in audience analysis, other kinds of research, planning, revising, editing, and proofreading. To get your thoughts into written words more rapidly, you'll need to shut down the inner voice that criticizes each syllable as you squeeze it out. For most of us, that voice is so dominant that it takes deliberate effort to silence it. Here are a few techniques you can try:

- **Beat the Clock**. Set a timer for a certain block of time and produce as many words as you can during that period. Turn off your Quality Assurance monitor completely during this time so that you concentrate only on output. (You'll also need to shut down your e-mail and other distractions, such as interruptions from your team.) When you produce at this level of intensity, you can probably work for no more than 30 to 90 minutes at a time, so be reasonable about the time goal you set for yourself.

- **Pomodoro Technique**. Italian developer Francesco Cirillo advocates for a variation on Beat the Clock that applies to any task. Using his technique, you work in 25-minute sprints with 5-minute rest periods in between.

  Pomodoro means tomato in Italian, referring to the shape of the kitchen timer Cirillo used when he first developed the method. If you don't happen to have a veggie-themed timer on hand, just download one of the several Pomodoro apps available for your computer or smartphone. (I like the free version of FocusKeeper.)

- **Invisible Writing.** That internal critic we all struggle with can't make snarky comments on your writing if they can't see the words you're producing. Try dimming your computer monitor and writing for short spurts without viewing the text you're turning out.

- **Daily Freewriting.** If you've ever challenged yourself to learn a second language, then you know that the only way to improve your fluency as a speaker is to practice as often as you can. The same goes for improving your writing fluency, the rate at which you're able to express your thoughts in written language.

  One of the best ways to work on your fluency is to practice *freewriting* for 10 minutes each morning. For this activity, I like to write by hand because I find the break from the computer screen liberating; the writing process literally feels different. I'd encourage you to experiment with using both the keyboard and the pen to find the method that feels most freeing for you.

When you're ready to freewrite, set a timer for 10 minutes and write without pausing for that entire time. If you get stuck, simply repeat the last word you've written until a new word comes. Or talk to yourself on paper about why you're feeling stuck. If you keep writing, the breakthrough will come. And if you practice freewriting daily, you'll retrain your brain to stop worrying about creating a perfect first draft and just get that draft done.

3. **Aim for a prototype, not a polished final product.** Take a page from Agile product development. Rather than investing a huge amount of time trying to create the perfect draft, assume that your first draft will be a rough prototype you'll need to re-engineer based on feedback.

Mike Cyr, cofounder and COO of Nanuk Technologies Inc., has learned first-hand the value of getting a minimum viable product to market quickly. Based on Canada's East Coast, Mike and his team create virtual reality tours for real estate developers. The developers use Nanuk's preprogrammed VR headsets to sell buyers properties before they're built.

Nanuk's first headset was, in Mike's words, a "kind of clunky" product, and Mike and his two partners had no idea how the market would react to it. So instead of trying to sell it, they treated it as a prototype and invited potential clients to give them feedback on how to improve it. That, says Mike, was tough to do because it meant allowing people to "tear apart" what Nanuk had spent years building. But the gutsy strategy paid off. Nanuk received candid comments that enabled it to launch a product more attuned to customer needs. And they established strong relationships with the people who provided feedback, who became collaborators in the development process.

Mike's advice about building innovative solutions applies equally well to creating writing: "Don't make it perfect. Just ship it." If you don't get your early product out to the market and brave the criticism, he says, you're not going to end up with a winning product: "At the end of the day, we're building a product for our customers, not ourselves."

In the same way, the writing you're creating is for your readers, not yourself. Treat your first version of any document as a prototype, and get feedback on it from your audience as soon as you can. By approaching writing as a collaborative, iterative process, you'll show your audience that you're truly invested in developing a relationship with them, not just talking at them in print.

Polishing the Final Product

When the product you're creating is a document, you can't always follow the Nanuk approach and share your draft with your customer or client (though you may be surprised to discover that there are many situations when the risk of sharing a draft weighs less than the risk of presenting a polished document without any audience input). But treating your draft as a prototype ensures that you allow ample time for the phase that follows prototyping—rework.

You can simplify and speed up rewriting by tackling it in three separate steps. (When you try to do all three at once, it's easy to get overwhelmed and lose your focus.) Table 1.4 describes each step and lists questions you can ask to coach yourself through each stage.

Leverage Your Personal Strengths

As you try out the tips and techniques I've shared with you, pay careful attention to what works—and what doesn't work—for you and your team. The surest way to gum up your writing process is to force yourself to follow routines that don't align with your personality or working style.

For instance, not everyone benefits from outlining. In fact, many writers produce better-organized writing without spending a lot of time crafting a detailed writing plan. So don't force yourself to follow the model outline your tenth-grade teacher gave you if it's not working for you. As an innovator, you know that inventiveness can follow an unpredictable path. Why should you pre-judge how you'll get a piece of writing from concept to delivery-ready?

Focus on your audience, commit to observing and refining your writing habits, and you'll soon evolve your own effective process for producing Change-Maker writing that makes great things happen.

Table 1.4 *Stages of rewriting*

Stage of rewriting	Areas of focus	Self-coaching questions
Revision	• Clarity of main ideas • Document structure • Depth of thought	1. What is my document's key message? Is it clearly stated near the beginning of the document? 2. Have I clearly connected each main idea to the document's key message so it's obvious how they develop it? 3. Have I supported my main ideas with evidence my audience will find compelling, (such as quotes, facts and figures, case studies, and examples)? 4. Is it easy for the reader to follow the logical flow of my document? 5. Have I missed any key aspect of my topic that my target audience will be expecting the document to address? 6. How might someone argue against my ideas? Have I answered anticipated objections? 7. Are there any parts of my document where my target reader might find the explanation or argument unclear or undeveloped?
Editing	• Clarity and correctness of sentences • Writing style • Graphic design	1. Are my sentences and paragraphs easy to follow? Does one sentence lead logically to the next? 2. Do my sentences accurately convey my intended meaning? 3. Are my sentences punctuated correctly? 4. Have I used a conversational style and simple language? 5. Does the writing style embody the company brand? 6. Are page layouts uncluttered and easy to read? 7. Have I used elements of graphic design, such as bulleted lists and tables, wherever possible?
Proofreading	• Typos • Inconsistent formatting	1. Have I run a spell checker? 2. Have I checked for single lines of text at the top and bottom of pages (widows and orphans)? 3. Have I inserted and checked page numbering? 4. Have I used fonts and colors consistently throughout the document?

Checklist for Change-Maker Writing

❑ Identify the target audience.

❑ Assess the audience's knowledge level.

❑ Probe the audience's fears.

❑ Explore the audience's aspirations.

❑ Describe the audience's values.

❑ Make informed design decisions about content, structure, style, and word choice (using the Change-Maker Writing Design Questions).

❑ Revise the document, examining it for clarity of main ideas, structure, and depth of thought.

❑ Edit the document, assessing clarity and correctness of sentences, the writing style, and graphic design.

❑ Proofread the document, checking for typos and inconsistent formatting.

CHAPTER 2

Everyday E-mails

In the 1998 romantic comedy *You've Got Mail*, the heroine, Kathleen, gasps with anticipation when the mailbox icon pops up on her computer screen, announcing a new message from an anonymous online love interest. Ironically, the man sending the messages, Joe, is a business competitor Kathleen can't stand in person. The movie's plot, which now seems rather quaint, depends on the contrast between the way Kathleen and Joe come across through their e-mails and the way they appear to each other in "real life."

Today, the film's premise has lost its novelty; with e-mails flooding our inboxes, few of us jump for joy every time we hear a notification chime. And many of us now spend so much time online that we've become desensitized to the differences between e-mail and live conversation. But those differences still exist, and skilled communicators pay close attention to them.

Even if you're not thinking about it, each time you write an e-mail message, you're creating an online persona, for yourself and your organization. Your words, sentences, and paragraphs work together to create an impression of your personal character and your company brand. Your e-mail persona embodies your personal leadership style as you attempt to persuade your reader or readers to take a particular course of action.

"Action" is the key word to keep in mind because *the only reason for writing an e-mail is to persuade the recipient to take a specific action*. If you find yourself typing away with no request for action in mind, then stop wasting your time and prevent yourself from wasting your reader's time. No action, no e-mail. Period.

(BTW, before you ask…yes, this guideline applies to FYI messages. When you write an FYI e-mail, it should be clear why you're sharing the information and how you expect the reader to use it. You're asking them to remember and record the information for a particular purpose, not just broadcasting information that may or may not be relevant to them.)

Because an e-mail message always drives toward a desired action, it's helpful to think about the various kinds of e-mails you write in terms of the different actions you want to happen. While you may write hundreds of e-mails in a week to a variety of audiences, many of those messages likely fall into one of these five common action categories:

1. Arrange a networking meeting
2. Get information
3. Start a business development conversation
4. Move a business development conversation to the next stage
5. Convince the reader to accept negative news

In each of these situations, your ability to persuade your reader depends largely on (1) how you organize your message and (2) how skilfully you address the interests and values that guide their behavior. While I can't offer you cookie-cutter templates to fit every writing challenge, here are some structural guidelines to help you achieve each of the five actions just listed.

E-mail Action #1: Arrange a Networking Meeting

When you're reaching out to someone you don't know, every sentence you write must aim to engage the reader. While the e-mail needs to be brief, take the time you need to introduce yourself properly and pique your reader's interest.

To grab and keep your audience's attention, you must answer five questions for them:

1. Who are you?
2. Why are you contacting me?
3. Why should I care?
4. What do you want from me?
5. How do I reply to you?

Here's an example of a networking e-mail to a stranger, asking for a conversation over coffee, in which you can see all five questions answered (Figure 2.1).

Whenever possible, start an e-mail by mentioning something you and your reader have in common. Here, a familiar name should grab Raina's attention.

If you don't have a name to drop, start by introducing yourself and stating your reason for writing.

It's clear what Jason is looking for, a casual conversation over coffee, and the time frame he has in mind. His request is phrased as a direct question.

If he were looking for a phone meeting, it would be good to put a time limit on the conversation. For example: Would you have time for a 20-minute call one afternoon next week?

Jason gives Raina multiple options for contacting him. His e-mail signature also lists all his contact details.

SUBJECT: Helping retailers take advantage of new technology

Raina,

Susan Charmer suggested I contact you because I'm launching a consulting company to help retailers take advantage of emerging technologies. My name is Jason Bercelli, and I have 12 years of experience working as a senior consultant for the Montreal-based technology firm Compucite. I've recently moved to Massachusetts and am eager to connect with other professionals who work in the retail innovation space.

From what Susan has told me about your augmented reality app, it sounds like we are serving a similar client base and helping retailers solve similar problems. I'd be interested to learn more about your company and the kinds of solutions you provide.

Would you be free to meet for coffee one day this week or next? I'm normally in Boston on Thursdays, and right now my calendar is clear for the afternoon of the 12th and the 19th.

The best way to reach me these days is by e-mail or by phone (voice or text) at 514-765-8956. I look forward to hearing from you soon.

Regards,
Jason

Jason Bercelli
Founder, Axia Consulting
www.axiaconsult.com
jason@axiaconsult.com
514-765-8956

The subject line includes a topic the reader cares about.

Jason makes it clear why he's writing. The phrase "eager to connect" creates positive emotional energy.

This paragraph shows Raina why she should care about Jason and his request. Meeting with Jason is an opportunity to share information about her products with someone who could pass the word along to potential customers.

If you can't think of a direct benefit the reader would gain by speaking with you, pitch them on the value of the work you're doing and explain how and why their insight would be helpful. (In other words, generate the intangible benefits associated with acting as a mentor.)

Figure 2.1 Networking e-mail

E-mail Action #2: Get Information

Asking someone to give you information means asking them to do work. Depending on the complexity of your request, they may need to hunt for the information, get permission to share it, summarize it, and/or select key parts of the information relevant to your situation. And then, of course, they have to write the e-mail replying to you.

Because of the effort involved, even a straightforward request must be persuasive. You may think that answering your e-mail is just part of the reader's job. But at any given moment, your audience is almost certainly dealing with a stack of requests. Your challenge is to make sure that yours goes to the top of the pile, and that means convincing your reader of two things: (1) that your request merits their prompt attention, and (2) that the action you're asking for will be easy for them to take.

An e-mail requesting information must motivate a response by answering the following five questions for the reader:

1. Who are you?
2. Why should I care about what you want?
3. What, exactly, do you want?
4. When do you want it?
5. How will your help matter?

A persuasive request for information doesn't necessarily have to tackle the questions in the order listed, but it should address them all in as brief a message as possible. It should also state the desired outcome of the message explicitly, as a direct question.

In other words, if you want someone to give you a piece of information, then ask for it. Don't imply your request; use a direct question, punctuated with a question mark, to trigger a response.

Consider the following two statements of a question, one implied and one direct. Which one would you be most likely to reply to?

- I was wondering if you could send me a copy of the proposal we wrote for Andrews Inc. last spring.
- Could you please send me a copy of the proposal we wrote for Andrews Inc. last spring?

Most people would choose the second option, and that's been validated by empirical research. A study of e-mail habits in a Norwegian telecommunications company found that 66 percent of messages that made a request provoked a response, but only 35 percent of e-mails that did not make a request got a reply.[1]

---

[1] K. Skovholt and J. Svennevig. 2013. "Responses and Non-responses in Workplace Emails." In *Handbook of the Pragmatics of Computer-Mediated Communication*, eds. S. Herring and T. Virtanen (Berlin, Germany: Mouton de Gruyter), pp. 581–603. https://www.researchgate.net/publication/275958714_Skovholt_K_Svennevig_J_2013_Responses_and_Non-responses_in_Workplace_Emails_I_S_Herring_D_Stein_T_Virtanen_Eds_Handbook_of_the_Pragmatics_of_Computer-Mediated_Communication_Mouton_de_Gruyter_581-603.

In a spoken conversation, when someone asks us a question, we're conditioned to respond. Make that knee-jerk reaction work for you by phrasing your requests as real asks, not wonderings. Remember that the question mark serves as a powerful visual cue to trigger a quick response.

Here's an example of a persuasive e-mail requesting information. Notice that it phrases the request as a direct question and that it motivates the reader by answering all of the five questions listed above (Figure 2.2):

The subject line provides specific context so the reader immediately sees why the message is important. In this case, because the information is required quickly, the subject line also provides a timeline.

Some writers like to flag time-sensitive requests for information as "urgent." However, what's urgent in your eyes may not qualify as urgent in the reader's eyes. Context and a timeline show why the request is urgent, giving the reader specific reasons to pay attention to the message.

The rationale for the timeline is explained here, and the request is stated as a direct question, emphasized in bold. Note that Geoff is definite about what he wants: access to the complete study, not just a particular data set.

SUBJECT: Data for Miller Avionics proposal needed for February 4

Hi Geoff,

As you know, Harry and I are working on the draft proposal for Miller Avionics, which is due next Thursday (February 12). To make a compelling business case, we need to summarize the flight safety data that Janet and Rob gathered through their study with the University of Utah last fall.

I believe that you have access to the drive where the study findings are stored. Normally, I'd ask Janet for access, but she's out sick this week, and Rob, as you know, is out of pocket while he's in Alaska.

I need the data by Wednesday so I can get the draft proposal to Sid in time for him to review and polish it. **Would you please send me the direct link to the safety study findings (the entire study) by EOD tomorrow?**

Thanks so much for your help! The Miller project would be an exciting growth opportunity for all of us, and the better our data, the better our chance of success.

If you have any questions, the best way to reach me today is Slack because I'll be in and out of meetings till 4.

Dieter

Geoff identifies himself in relation to a project the reader is aware of.

Geoff answers the question "Why should I care?" by positioning his request in terms of the success of the project the reader is already aware of and recognizes as important. In this case, since the audience is already aware of the importance of the project, a brief mention of the context does the job. In other situations, you may need to elaborate and explain the significance of the task or project you're working on.

This paragraph provides a rationale for the request, which is not part of the reader's routine work. It also makes it sound as if the requested action will be easy for the reader to perform: he already has access to the drive where the data is stored.

The thank-you shows how the reader's help is significant. We all want to feel valued, and a little appreciation can go a long way toward motivating a response.

Always make it easy for your reader to follow up with you if any more information is needed for them to fulfill your request.

Figure 2.2 E-mail requesting information

E-mail Action #3: Set Up a Discovery Conversation

Now that you know how to craft an e-mail to request a networking meeting, you're already halfway to writing a persuasive message to ask for a more focused kind of meeting, a *discovery conversation*. A discovery conversation is more than a get-to-know-you chat. It gives you and a potential client or partner the opportunity to explore the possibility of developing a business relationship. The goal is for you to find out, as much as you can, about the other party's interests and needs so you can determine whether they might be a good candidate for the products and services or the investment opportunity you have to offer.

Most business development professionals use a combination of phone and e-mail when they're trying to arrange a discovery conversation. Some like to make the first contact by phone and then follow up with an e-mail, providing additional information and perhaps including a one-pager summarizing their products and services. (We'll cover tips for crafting compelling one-pagers in Part IV.) Others prefer to reach out first via e-mail and then follow up with a voicemail message.

In his prospecting for Nanuk Technologies, Mike Cyr tends to start with e-mail because the written form allows him to begin cultivating a relationship through "meticulously" worded messages. In his experience, the value of e-mail comes through what many perceive as its liability—it can sit in the recipient's inbox until the reader is ready to give it their full attention. A phone call, Mike says, almost always interrupts the prospect while they're in the middle of a task, when the person's main goal is to get off the phone as quickly as possible. An e-mail, on the other hand, speaks to the prospect when they've chosen to hear what it has to say.

To capture and keep the reader's attention, that initial message must pique the reader's curiosity and give them what Mike calls an "incentive" for agreeing to a meeting. In that sense, an e-mail requesting a discovery conversation functions as a kind of mini pitch. You're not selling your product or service, but you are selling the value of engaging with you. It's critical, then, that the persona you create comes across as friendly, professional, and sincerely focused on the reader's best interests.

This is the kind of situation in which it pays to watch your pronouns. To paraphrase John F. Kennedy, ask not what your reader can do for you; ask what you can do for your reader. Avoid overloading your message with statements beginning with "I," such as "I wanted to let you know…" or "I'd like to arrange a meeting…" Instead, from the first sentence to your closing, keep the focus on the reader and the reasons why they should invest their precious time in meeting with you.

Here's an example of a prospecting e-mail requesting an initial conversation with a new business contact. As you read through it, notice how it anticipates and answers seven questions that are likely to come up in the reader's mind (Figure 2.3):

1. Who are you?
2. Why should I care about what you have to say?
3. Why do you want to meet?
4. What will I get from the meeting?
5. What are your expectations for the meeting?
6. Why should I make time for this meeting now?
7. How do I reply to you?

The Importance of E-mail Persistence

A message that hits all seven of the above questions greatly increases your chances of getting a quick reply. But let's be real: in today's business environment, people seldom reply to the first e-mail or phone call from a stranger because their working lives are just too harried for them to deal with much beyond the immediately urgent. No matter how beautifully crafted your first e-mail is, the brutal fact is that you should expect to follow up on it with additional messages.

Each time I send an e-mail like the example you've just read, I put a note in my to-do list to follow up with a phone call two or three days later. In some situations, I may make up to five follow-up calls before I get a reply. When I finally do hear from the person I've been trying to reach, they often start the phone call or e-mail by thanking me for so diligently trying to connect with them.

Now, as Mike Cyr puts it, "there's a fine line between being persistent and being annoying." But you can win your prospect's attention by showing sincere interest in their organization. In his follow-up e-mails, Mike mentions details about the company's recent achievements, which he gleans from their website and press coverage. This kind of specificity shows the prospect you care about their goals and their success, and it pays off. "I'm always researching our prospects," explains Mike. "You've got to show them you've done your research so they'll give you the time of day."

SUBJECT: New material for eco-friendly furniture

Derek,

My name is Charlene Forrester. I'm Director of Business Development for SpudBoard Inc., a Boise-based company that manufactures environment-friendly particle board from potato peels.

Charlene starts by identifying herself and explaining what her company does.

Congratulations on yesterday's award for Idaho's Green Manufacturer of the Year! It's great to see a local company taking the lead in eco-innovation.

This paragraph shows that Charlene is interested in Derek's company. This personal touch helps to capture the reader's attention.

Like you, SpudBoard is also committed to reducing the furniture industry's carbon footprint. Our particle board is made entirely from potato peels that would otherwise end up in the landfill, and our production process runs on solar power and gray water. Because no toxic chemicals are used, the product is 100 percent organic and releases none of the harmful fumes that conventional particle board gives off.

Here, Charlene answers the question "Why should I care?" She identifies with the prospect, showing that SpudBoard and GreenBean share the same values and mission.

I would be curious to learn more about your manufacturing process and explore ways that SpudBoard might be able to help with your mission to develop earth-friendly ways of producing furniture. Would you have time for a 20-minute conversation one day next week?

I will be visiting the Columbus area on July 10 and 11 and could meet at your office on one of those days. Otherwise, I could meet by phone next Wednesday or Friday afternoon.

Here, Charlene creates a sense of urgency by stating specific times she will be in Derek's city.

If it would be easiest to work out a time by phone, you can reach me on my cell (by voice or text) at 208-954-3221. If you don't get a chance to reply by Tuesday, I'll circle back with you by phone.

Charlene makes it easy for Derek to reply to her and indicates how she'll follow up.

I look forward to hearing from you soon.

Regards,

Charlene

Charlene keeps the focus on the client and sets up a discovery conversation, not a sales call. She frames the conversation as an opportunity for the client; it offers them a chance to share their mission and explore possible benefits of collaborating with SpudBoard. Charlene also establishes clear expectations for the meeting. The purpose will be to learn and to explore, and the meeting will take just 20 minutes.

Figure 2.3 E-mail requesting a discovery conversation

E-mail Action #4: Move a Business Development Conversation to the Next Stage

Once you've met with a prospect for a discovery conversation, how do you nurture the relationship you've started to build? With great care.

A message following up on a meeting must cultivate the audience's trust, line by line. To do that, you must:

1. Express appreciation for the time the prospect invested in the meeting
2. Show how well you've listened during the meeting
3. Respond specifically to any requests for information
4. Recap key points of your conversation, including rebuttals of objections
5. Indicate the next step you'd like to see happen

Here's an example of a follow-up e-mail Charlene could send after her meeting with Derek (Figure 2.4):

SUBJECT: Continuing our conversation about eco-friendly particle board

Derek,

Thanks for taking the time to meet with me yesterday. I was fascinated to learn about the production process you're using with your new sofa line, especially your use of recycled T-shirts to make the cushion covers.

> In her opening paragraph, Charlene thanks the prospect and recalls a specific part of the conversation. She expresses genuine interest in the prospect's business.

You asked for some additional information about SpudBoard's durability. You'll find attached a white paper that describes how SpudBoard is made and lists some statistics from our recent pressure testing. As you'll see on page 6, SpudBoard outperforms conventional particle board and balsa wood on several measures.

> Charlene responds to Derek's request for information—and she makes it easy for him to find exactly the data he's looking for.

> A recap of the discussion sets up another conversation as a logical step.

As we discussed, SpudBoard and GreenBean could partner up in a few different ways, but the simplest, most low-risk option would be a small pilot project involving your newest sofa model. I've spoken with our CEO, Matthys Erikson, and he's eager to explore that possibility.

> The request for a meeting states a clear purpose for the call, moving the prospect toward a specific next step.

Would you be available for a call next week to flesh out the concept of a pilot project? Right now, Matt and I have availability on Thursday afternoon and Friday morning.

Looking forward to continuing our conversation,

Charlene

Figure 2.4 E-mail following up on a meeting

E-mail Action #5: Convince the Reader to Accept Negative News

It's so challenging to deliver bad news via e-mail that I often advise people to pick up the phone or arrange a face-to-face conversation instead. But many situations require us to take the tough road and put negative news in writing. Perhaps the message is time-sensitive, and we need to get it to someone who's hard to reach by phone, or maybe we need a written record for our files. Whatever the situation, many of us find ourselves writing "bad news messages" more often than we'd like.

And sometimes we're creating such messages without acknowledging them as such. "Bad news" isn't always earth-shattering. Any time you need to communicate ideas or information your audience don't want to hear, you're delivering bad news. Everyday kinds of negative messages include e-mails that announce a delay, refuse a request, or correct a misunderstanding. Whether you need to tell a client you'll be sending a major deliverable a week late or you simply need to clarify a minor point with a team member, such messages always deserve careful attention because they can easily misfire.

Fortunately, a simple five-point structure removes much of the risk involved in bearing bad news:

1. Gentle lead-in—a brief, honest statement that helps prepare the audience for the bad news to come
2. Reason for the bad news—a clear rationale that paves a logical path toward the bad news
3. The bad news—a crystal-clear statement of the negative message
4. Reasonable alternative—a viable solution the audience could consider as a way to achieve their goals
5. Genuine, compassionate closing—a sincere sign-off that fosters goodwill

Step-by-step, this structure guides the reader through a process of anticipating, absorbing, and accepting the bad news.

The five steps I've outlined differ from the so-called "sandwich method," which follows a misleading structure of good news/bad news/positive close. Remember that the goal of any e-mail is to persuade the reader to take action. Merely creating a positive vibe won't persuade the reader to do what you want them to do and, in fact, may confuse them.

A far smarter strategy is to focus your message on two action-oriented outcomes: you want your audience to (1) accept your bad news and (2) cooperate with you by following whatever alternative steps you've proposed.

Below is an example of a persuasive bad news message. Be sure to check out the annotations because they include notes on some of the common mistakes people make in applying this structure (Figure 2.5).

2. Reason for the bad news. Here's the undisputable rationale for the bad news, stated plainly and succinctly, and also without blame: the foremen have been unavailable.

Common mistakes: Omitting the rationale, providing a weak rationale (such as "it's company policy"), or placing the rationale after the bad news.

3. The bad news. This is stated, explicitly.

Common mistake: Failing to state the bad news clearly so that the reader cannot grasp its significance.

Whenever you're stating a problem, be sure to provide the date by which you expect to resolve it. That way, you give your audience all the information they need in order to weigh the alternative you present.

1. Gentle lead-in. The opening paragraph provides context for the message and provides a gentle, short lead-in to the bad news. Note that there is no apology, no excuse, and no blaming. In some situations, you may need to apologize, but here the reason for the delay is the weather, which no one can control.

Common mistake: Making the introduction too long and going out of the way to be overly positive or flattering. Keep it short and sincere.

4. Reasonable alternative. This is a viable alternative, which gives Pat a legitimate choice and a sense of control.

Common mistakes: Omitting an alternative (an approach that can make the audience feel powerless and frustrated) or presenting an alternative that's not really workable.

5. Genuine, compassionate closing. This action-oriented ending emphasizes the audience's ability to choose the path forward and creates a positive vision. The tone is professional but also warm and personal.

Common mistake: Using a "canned" ending, such as "Thanks for your patience" or "Trusting this will suffice."

SUBJECT: Update on app customization

Hi Pat,

As you know, Benji has been working diligently with three of your Hamilton foremen to gather the site data we need to customize Habitat for Barclay Construction. As you're also aware, the streak of fine weather we've had over the past 10 days has kept the Hamilton crews working nonstop.

Because the foremen have had no downtime since May 2, we've been unable to customize Habitat to the degree we normally do. We're missing some information about the ways your foremen liaise with the engineering team, and the automatic meeting scheduler will not work properly without that.

We expect to meet with the foremen next Wednesday (May 21) to gather the missing information. Then we'll need a week after that to finish completely customizing the app.

I realize that you were hoping to use Habitat at the new shopping center site starting next week. Currently, the app is fully functional except for the automatic scheduling feature. If you'd prefer, we could release it to you now as is, with a manual option for scheduling meetings. We could then implement the fully customized app as an upgrade before the end of the month.

Please let me know how you'd like to proceed. The developers and I are eager to see Habitat in the hands of your team as soon as possible so you can start taking advantage of the many ways it will make communication easier for your crews, even during their busiest periods.

Kim

Figure 2.5 Bad news e-mail

Creating Your Own E-mail Action Templates

You now have models you can use to lead e-mail readers toward five different kinds of business actions. As you use the models in your business, you may be able to adapt them and produce more specific templates to suit particular situations and audiences. For instance, you might create one bad news template for refusing customer requests for a refund and a second bad news template for letting a customer know about a delay caused by a supplier issue.

Whatever your circumstances and whoever your audience, keep in mind the persona you want to create through your e-mail writing and the result or results you want to see happen. If you do that, you'll find that e-mail becomes a tool not just for sharing information but also for asserting your personal style of leadership, forging positive relationships, and building trust.

Checklist for Everyday E-mail Actions

Persuasive e-mails anticipate the key questions readers need you to answer so they can understand your message and take the action you want them to take. This checklist includes a set of questions for each of the five kinds of e-mails explored in this chapter. I encourage you to add new question sets as you create your own e-mail templates customized to your business activities.

E-mail Action #1: Arrange a Networking Meeting
- ❑ Who are you?
- ❑ Why are you contacting me?
- ❑ Why should I care?
- ❑ What do you want from me?
- ❑ How do I reply to you?

E-mail Action #2: Get Information
- ❑ Who are you?
- ❑ Why should I care about what you want?
- ❑ What, exactly, do you want?
- ❑ When do you want it?
- ❑ How will your help matter?

E-mail Action #3: Set Up a Discovery Conversation
- ❑ Who are you?
- ❑ Why should I care about what you have to say?
- ❑ Why do you want to meet?
- ❑ What will I get from the meeting?
- ❑ What are your expectations for the meeting?
- ❑ Why should I make time for this meeting now?
- ❑ How do I reply to you?

E-mail Action #4: Move a Business Development Conversation to the Next Stage

- ❑ Express appreciation for the time the prospect invested in the meeting.
- ❑ Show how well you've listened during the meeting.
- ❑ Respond specifically to any requests for information.
- ❑ Recap key points of your conversation, including rebuttals of objections.
- ❑ Indicate the next step you'd like to see happen.

E-mail Action #5: Convince the Reader to Accept Negative News

- ❑ Gentle lead-in—a brief, honest statement that helps prepare the audience for the bad news to come
- ❑ Reason for the bad news—a clear rationale that paves a logical path toward the bad news
- ❑ The bad news—a crystal-clear statement of the negative message
- ❑ Reasonable alternative—a viable solution the audience could consider as a way to achieve their goals
- ❑ Genuine, compassionate closing—a sincere sign-off that fosters goodwill

CHAPTER 3

Marketing E-mails

People say data is the new currency of business, but I beg to differ. Certainly, data has become the resource fueling many marketing, production, and other business activities. But in a world awash in data, *trust* has become the new currency.

In this chapter, you'll learn how to build trust through e-mail marketing that delivers consistent value to your clients or customers. We'll zero in on two particular types of marketing e-mails: newsletters and sales letters. We'll also explore seven general principles to help you build trust through e-mail marketing, and we'll examine the art of creating a compelling subject line, the finishing touch without which the most finely crafted e-mail is worthless.

How Deep Is Your Trust Fund?

As I write this, more than 100 million people in the United States and Canada are reeling from a data breach at Capital One. The breach compromised names, addresses, e-mails, credit scores, Social Security numbers, and bank accounts. Just a little over a month ago, a similar incident happened in a Canadian credit union, Desjardins Group. That breach exposed the personal data of almost three million people, causing one irate customer to launch a petition asking the Canadian government to reissue Social Insurance numbers. At last count, more than 75,000 people had signed the petition.[1]

---

[1] CBC (based on a report by David Rémaillard). July 7, 2019. "Thousands of Desjardins Members Sign Petition Demanding New SINs," *CBC website*. https://www.cbc.ca/news/canada/montreal/desjardins-members-new-social-insurance-numbers-1.5202999.

The Capital One and Desjardins privacy scandals have created tsunami-sized shock waves because financial institutions have traditionally enjoyed the reputation of being highly trustworthy businesses. Many of them can boast of long histories and generations of loyal clients. (Desjardins devotes a large section of its website to the company history and has turned the birthplace of its founder, Alphonse Desjardin, into a museum.) Unlike startups, organizations in the financial sector have traditionally had a large "trust fund" they could draw upon when interacting with the market.

I take the notion of "trust fund" from Stephen Covey, who talks about trust as an accumulation of positive emotional credits we gain when we act in trustworthy ways. Every time I promise a client a document by a certain date and then deliver it on time, I earn a trust credit with them. In Covey's terms, I make a "deposit" into an "Emotional Bank Account."[2] On the flip side, when I show impatience during a meeting or let a project detail slip, I withdraw funds from the account. Relationships deepen when you make more deposits than withdrawals and do so both frequently and consistently.

When you approach a potential client or customer, certain qualities about your company give you a starting balance in your trust account. If, for instance, you can point to 120 years of excellence in customer service or a global customer base of millions of people, you'll automatically begin with a healthy balance in your trust fund. But if you're an innovative entrepreneur with relatively unknown products or services, you'll have to work hard to establish even a minimal balance in your trust fund.

E-mail marketing gives you a powerful vehicle for making trust deposits with your target audience. With the explosion of social media, you might think of e-mail as a rather old-fashioned way to reach your audience. But, to borrow one of Mark Twain's quips, the rumor of e-mail's death has been greatly exaggerated. Whereas social media is becoming less

---

[2]S. Covey. 2013. *The Seven Habits of Highly Effective People: Powerful Lessons in Personal Change*. 25th anniversary ed. (New York, NY: Rosetta Books), "Paradigms of Interdependence," Kindle.

and less about social connection and more about "social entertainment,"[3] e-mail allows you to nurture a prospect's relationship with your brand, cultivate trust, and persuade the prospect to become a paying customer.

Why E-mail Still Matters in the Age of Social Selling

According to GlobalWebIndex, a market research firm focused on social media usage, in the first quarter of 2019, these were the top four reasons people engage in social media:

- "To stay up-to-date with news and current events"
- "To stay in touch with what my friends are doing"
- "To find funny or entertaining content"
- "To fill up spare time"

Despite all the hoopla over social selling as the next phase of e-commerce, it seems that most people are engaging with public platforms such as Facebook and Instagram for reasons that are neither social nor sales-oriented. Much of the personal information-sharing that happens online is now occurring through private messaging apps and e-mail, and people are looking to mainstream social media for the same kind of content they look to mainstream media outlets to provide: news stories and cheap entertainment.[4]

In contrast, people subscribe to e-mail lists so they can engage with your brand in deeper ways. Typically, they want to learn from you and about you. They're not looking for a giggle over a Grumpy Cat video; they want you to provide them with helpful content they can put to practical use. When you give them that content, you're fulfilling an implied

---

[3]GlobalWebIndex. 2019. "Social: GlobalWebIndex's Flagship Report on the Latest Trends in Social Media," p. 3. https://www.globalwebindex.com/hubfs/Downloads/2019%20 Q1%20Social%20Flagship%20Report.pdf?utm_campaign=Social%20report%20 July%202019&utm_source=hs_automation&utm_medium=e-mail&utm_con-tent=74226065&_hsenc=p2ANqtz-8hAe1M2SewJ-ZkcZDE7ZiyEP2cyojPG9S-50l0_LT9PEH988ukfKXkrcGf3jz3vfAVdbX1mwwOE9w4olPKssky6pqXSg&_hsmi=74226065.
[4]GlobalWebIndex, 2019, pp. 11–12.

promise. That means you automatically make a deposit in your audience's trust account, and you also make them curious about what else you might have to offer them.

Trust and the curiosity it fosters help explain why e-mail newsletters tend to connect with a greater proportion of an audience than social media posts do. Antoine Bonicalzi is marketing director at Cyberimpact, a company that offers e-mail marketing software tailored to Canada's stringent privacy regulations. He explains the difference between e-mail marketing and social media marketing this way:

> If you have 1,000 e-mail subscribers and you send out a newsletter, you can have 20, 30, 40, 50, even 60 percent or more of that 1,000 people open your e-mail and read what you have to say. If you're posting on social media, and you have 1,000 fans of your business page, you're lucky to have 5 or 10% of them actually seeing your post because of the social algorithm. And in someone's feed, you're competing with their friends, their family, cute dog pictures, and all that.

In Antoine's view, e-mail and social media do two very different things. He uses social media the way he once would have used print advertising: to attract the attention of people who don't know the Cyberimpact brand. He uses e-mail for a different purpose: to nurture relationships with people who already know his brand. Those are people who've already opened a "trust account" with you, and e-mail marketing gives you an easy way to make regular deposits to it.

The two main forms of e-mail marketing messages, e-mail newsletters and sales e-mails, both depend on trust-building strategies, but they follow different structures. We'll start with newsletters because, once you get past a few technical requirements, you'll find they're straightforward messages to produce. With a little practice, you'll soon be able to turn out an engaging weekly message in less than an hour. As you develop confidence and greater writing fluency, you might even match the speed of business coach Mark Silver, who says he can write a news-letter in just 12 minutes![5]

Nuts and Bolts of E-mail Newsletters

Contrary to entrepreneurial myth, you can craft compelling e-mail marketing messages without the services of a professional copywriter and without elaborate technology. To get started, you do, though, need to make practical decisions in the following five areas:

1. **Technology**—The "tech" you choose doesn't need to be complicated, but working with e-mail marketing software from the beginning will make your life decidedly less complicated down the road. Examples of such software include Cyberimpact, MailChimp, Constant Contact, and Mad Mimi, to name just a few. These applications make it easy for you to build your e-mail mailing list, send messages to certain segments of the list, pre-schedule e-mail sequences, and track delivery and opening rates. They also allow you to add visuals, including brand imagery, to your messages.

2. **Branding**—Each e-mail you send becomes an ambassador of your brand. When a message shows up in someone's inbox, it's representing your business, so you want it to be impeccably groomed. Take time to create a basic template that uses your brand palette, logo, and fonts. Also consider how you'll use images, such as stock photos or pictures of products, to create visual appeal. Create simple design guidelines you can apply consistently—because consistency builds trust.

   Along with your visual brand, create guidelines for your brand voice. What kind of personality will your e-mails emanate? (For help defining your brand voice, check out the tips in Chapter 10.)

3. **Regulations**—The privacy laws governing e-mail are continually evolving, so your first step is to determine the current regulations

---

[5]M. Silver. August 28, 2019. "Reducing Article Writing from 4 hours to 12 minutes," *Heart of Business blog*. https://www.heartofbusiness.com/2019/reducing-article-writing-from-4-hours-to-12-minutes/.

that apply in your geographical region and industry. (Keep in mind that "geographical region" may mean where you do business or where your servers are located, or both.)

Canada has some of the toughest e-mail legislation in the world, Canada's Anti-Spam Law, or CASL.[6] It requires "express consent" or a "valid implied consent" for commercial e-mails, and organizations that fail to follow the rules can be fined up to $10 million. In the United States, the CAN-SPAM[7] Act also places limitations on the way businesses can use e-mail, and in Europe the General Data Protection Regulation applies to e-mail as well as other online transactions.[8]

Wherever your business is based, before you send your first newsletter, make sure that you've configured your e-mail marketing software to comply with all the global regulations that could apply to both you and your audience.

4. **Frequency of contact.** Consistency, we've seen, builds trust because it makes you predictable and reliable. Decide how often you'll reach out to your e-mail list and stick with that schedule.

Not sure how much e-mail communication you have capacity to create, deliver, and monitor? Start small, with a monthly or bi-weekly message to your list. Once you're sure you can handle that, you can increase the frequency of contact.

Creating Premium Newsletter Content

While you can use e-mail simply to announce special events and promotions, those kinds of messages don't do much to grow your trust fund.

---

[6]Canadian Radio-television and Telecommunications Commission. September 18, 2019. "Frequently Asked Questions about Canada's Anti-spam Legislation." https://crtc.gc.ca/eng/com500/faq500.htm.

[7]Federal Trade Commission. March, 2019. "CAN-SPAM Act: A Compliance Guide for Business." https://www.ftc.gov/tips-advice/business-center/guidance/can-spam-act-compliance-guide-business.

[8]European Commission. n.d. "Rules for Businesses and Organisations." https://ec.europa.eu/info/law/law-topic/data-protection/reform/rules-business-and-organisations_en, (accessed September 21, 2019).

To nourish the trust that people have placed in you by subscribing to your e-mail list, you need to give them *high-value content, unattached to a specific offer.* Position yourself as a knowledgeable, helpful mentor with expertise to share, and your generosity will reap you great returns.

Antoine thinks of e-mail marketing primarily as *content marketing.* He even encourages brands to become "their own media," which means sending e-mail newsletters that provide educational and informative content, not just promotional content. Picture a series of newsletter e-mails published as a single document. Ideally, that document looks more like a magazine than a stack of flyers.

As an example of a brand that uses e-mail newsletters to publish premium content, Antoine points to a Montreal mattress store. Their e-mails have the look and feel of a glossy lifestyle magazine. Instead of describing pocket coils and different versions of memory foam, they give tips for relaxing, getting a good night's sleep, and decorating your bedroom as a tranquil sanctuary. A person might subscribe to the e-mails for years without making a purchase. But when it comes time to replace an old mattress, we know which company will be trusted and top-of-mind.

The key to building that kind of trust, says Antoine, is to strike just the right balance between informative content and promotional content. If you're having a sales event, then, of course, let your newsletter readers know about it. But keep in mind the advice that Antoine gives to Cyberimpact clients: "You have to give to build trust, and you have to showcase your expertise. There's no better way to do that than by publishing and sending out informative content."

That doesn't mean that all the content you craft for your e-mail newsletter needs to be original content. You might use your newsletter as a vehicle to direct readers to your latest blog post or podcast, a free video series, or an upcoming free webinar. You might also use it to share carefully curated content you've gleaned from the Web.

When people open an e-mail from your company, you want them to feel as if they've just received a gift that was carefully chosen just for them. That gift can take many different forms. What matters is that it speaks directly to the audience's needs and gives them something they can use right away to help solve a problem or make a positive change in their world.

For instance, let's say your company provides vermicomposters (worm composters) for small offices. Here's an example of what the content for a simple weekly newsletter might look like for your organization. The numbered notes point out aspects of the writing you might want to emulate in your own newsletters (Figure 3.1).

FIVE SMALL CHANGES TO CUT YOUR OFFICE PAPER USE IN HALF

When office blue bins were first introduced back in the 1990s, everyone expected them to dramatically reduce paper waste. Boy, were we wrong!

A recent study from The New Hampshire Sustainability Institute (NHSI) shows that office blue bins do nothing to cut back on paper use. In fact, they actually encourage people to use more paper. Instead of restricting their printing, office workers tend to print more pages when they have access to a recycling receptacle.

If nature abhors a vacuum, an office abhors an empty collection bin. "The presence of a blue bin appears to create a psychological obligation to fill it," says industrial engineer Johanna Franklin, lead author of the NHSI's Report on Blue Bin Use for 2019. "So people don't think twice about printing. They feel like they're being a responsible corporate citizen by contributing to the blue bin."

It seems we need to look outside the blue box to find practical ways to reduce paper usage. Try some of these simple tips to change your relationship with the office printer and cut back on your personal paper use:

- **Use highlighting and annotation tools to mark up documents.** People who love highlighters love to print off documents so they can mark them up in a rainbow of colors. If that's you, experiment with some of the annotation tools available through apps such as GoodReads and Evernote. If you use a next-generation touchscreen computer or a tablet, you'll find there's little difference between the physical experience of marking up a document onscreen and the sensation of marking it up on paper.

- **Enlarge the viewing font when you're editing.** People tend to print out documents to edit them because reading from paper requires less effort than reading from a screen. But you can reduce onscreen reading effort by simply enlarging the font.

- **Split your viewing screen when you're revising.** Another common reason people print documents is so they can easily compare different sections of their writing when they're revising and rewriting. Most word processing programs, including Microsoft Word, make it easy for you to split your screen so you can view two parts of a document at once.

- **Pick up the phone or arrange a meeting.** If you find yourself printing off email threads because they've become long and complex, maybe it's time to arrange a phone call or meeting.

- **Explore what your tablet can do for you.** Most people use just 10% of the capabilities of any technology they interact with, so chances are you're underusing your iPad or Android tablet. Take an hour or two to explore its features, and you may be surprised to discover how many everyday tasks it can enable you to do paper-free.

Tree-based paper is one of the most carbon-intensive resources we use in our office life, so trying just one or two of these small changes could make a big difference to your overall environmental impact at work.

What's the biggest small change your office has made this month to improve sustainability? Share your success - join the VermiFresh Sustainability Group on Facebook!

Figure 3.1 Sample e-mail newsletter

1. Notice that the newsletter's subject doesn't stick to vermicom-posting. The newsletter provides educational, informative content that would appeal to an audience that's generally interested in issues associated with waste reduction and sustainability.
2. Notice the casual tone. A newsletter should sound conversational. Striking a friendly, approachable tone helps build trust. Antoine encourages e-mail writers to experiment with humor and think about how to bring a smile to the reader's day.
3. This reference to a scientific study showcases VermiFresh's expertise as a leader in sustainability.
4. Practical tips are numbered for easy reading.
5. A clear call to action directs readers to a next step: contributing to or joining the VermiFresh Facebook group. In another e-mail, the call to action might point readers to a website or a special offer.

As you can see from this example, your newsletter can be very simple—just a single article can do the job. If you'd like to create something a bit weightier, a common approach is to include a brief update, a customer success story, an educational article, and a description of a particular offering. If VermiFresh followed this format, here's what a table of contents for one of their newsletters might look like:

- Personal note from the CEO describing how she was inspired by a recent conversation with David Suzuki
- Customer success story: how an apartment building in Seattle cut out two garbage collection days a week by installing a VermiFresh bin on each floor
- Educational article: five small changes to cut your office paper use in half
- Description of an offering: forthcoming family-sized model on sale for pre-release price

As you brainstorm what your newsletter's table of contents might include, remember that your goal is not to create an encyclopedia on your industry. You're simply trying to give your audience bite-sized portions of high-value content that will whet their appetite for what you have to offer.

Combining Newsletter Information with Action

A strong e-mail newsletter can prove its worth through two important metrics: the click-to-open rate (the percentage of recipients who open the message) and the click-through rate (the percentage of recipients who click on a link in your message). Although the first metric tends to receive a lot of attention, the second metric may be even more significant because it shows how effectively your e-mail is persuading recipients to act on what they've read.

While an e-mail newsletter should mainly provide informative content, its ultimate goal is to nudge readers one small step closer to buying from you. The nudging happens through an explicit action step—a "call to action," or CTA—stated at the end of your newsletter.

In the VermiFresh example above, the CTA is "join the VermiFresh Sustainability Group on Facebook." Here are some other examples of typical CTAs you'll find at the end of e-mail newsletters:

- For more information, call us at...
- Curious to learn how our service can help you? Book your free discovery session.
- Check out our website at www...
- Like us on Facebook
- Let's connect on LinkedIn!
- Call today for your free assessment.
- Click here for a coupon that will give you 10 percent off your next purchase.

When you state your CTA, make sure it's specific and direct. A common mistake, Antoine says, is not spelling out the CTA clearly enough. "Don't be shy," he warns. "You cannot be too clear as to what the call to action is, the next step. At the end of your e-mail, people should know what you want them to do."

When Antoine sits own to write an e-mail newsletter, he always begins with the call to action in mind so that everything he writes aligns with the desired action. In the second kind of marketing e-mails we're going to examine, sales letters, alignment with the call to action becomes even more critical. As we'll see, sales letters follow a well-tested structure that leads the reader step-by-step down a path toward a purchase decision or an in-depth sales conversation.

Structuring Persuasive Sales E-mails

When you're writing an e-mail newsletter, it's best to operate by the mantra "less is more." But when you're crafting a sales letter, more is more. When you're writing with the aim of making a sale, you must make sure you provide all the information your prospect needs to make an informed buying decision.

If you printed out an effective e-mail sales letter, it would run to several pages, like the old-fashioned sales letters that used to arrive in the mailbox. In fact, the electronic medium has barely altered the form that direct mail copywriters have relied on for decades. To master the art of the e-mail sales letter, you simply need to master the well-tested structure that has supported sales-by-mail campaigns since before the era of *Mad Men.*

E-mail newsletters and sales letters work together as a powerful messaging team. An e-mail newsletter builds up your "trust account" with a prospect over time, through consistently delivering information the audience finds relevant and practical. An e-mail sales letter capitalizes that trust by inviting the audience to buy or to take a significant step toward a purchase, such as agreeing to a sales meeting or a discovery conversation.

It does that by taking the reader on a structured journey from skepticism toward belief and action. That journey follows predictable steps, using stories, in-depth description, testimonials, and FAQs to guide the reader along the path to commitment.

Following is an example of copy for an e-mail sales letter showing the 10 different steps (Figure 3.2). As you read through each section of the copy, consider what "raw material" you could draw on to structure a similar journey for your audience. What customer stories, personal experiences, case studies, and testimonials might you use to create a letter that will move your readers to buy from you? (For a summary of the 10 steps in the sales letter journey, see the Sales Letter Checklist at the end of this chapter.)

Dear Anne-Marie,

Imagine having a real conversation with your Down's Syndrome child. Give your child the gift of speech through a new iPad app, SpeakMee.

You wouldn't think that *Old MacDonald's Farm* could reduce a grown woman to tears. But as Sharon Blakeny listens to her 7-year-old daughter Jemma gleefully shout out the name of each animal on the iPad screen, she has to dab at the corner of her eye with her sweater sleeve.

You see, Jemma has Down's Syndrome, and just 6 months ago, she couldn't pronounce her name, let alone say "Porky Pig" or "Speckled Hen." Jemma's speech difficulties were so severe that her speech pathologist said she doubted Jemma would ever be able to do more than make guttural sounds.

Then Sharon and Jemma discovered **SpeakMee, a revolutionary new iPad app that teaches children with speech challenges how to enunciate clearly.** Today, Jemma can pronounce more than 350 words. Besides naming farm animals, she can say what we want for breakfast, ask her brother to pass her a toy, and tell her mom, "I love you."

SpeakMee will debut in the Apple App Store next month, and you and your child could be among the first to benefit from this life-changing software. I'm writing to personally invite you to take advantage of a **special early-bird offer** we're offering just to the folks who subscribe to our e-mail list.

1. **Internal headline.** Just below your personalized greeting, insert a headline to grab the audience's attention and hint at the promise of your offer.

2. **Story illustrating the problem your solution solves.** A story pulls readers into the e-mail by tugging on their emotions. Use empathy to show that you identify with and understand your reader's challenges.

Even though SpeakMee is a technical product with many sophisticated features, the opening of the letter is not the place to delve into those. The first task is to "hook" the reader emotionally because only once they're engaged with the writing will they be interested in considering technical details.

"I never thought I'd be able to have a conversation with my daughter. And now I think she will have so many opportunities I couldn't even have imagined a year ago. We have far fewer temper tantrums now that she can express herself. And we're starting the process of enrolling her in a school-readiness program, which is something that seemed totally out of reach before we started using SpeakMee."

Sharon Blakeny

3. **Testimonial.** Endorsements and case studies from real people who've used your product and benefited from it should, as you'll see, appear throughout the letter. It's a good idea to place one testimonial near the beginning as it's a great way to start building trust in you and your organization.

Figure 3.2 Sample sales e-mail

Not Just Another Talking Tutor

Before investing in SpeakMee, Sharon and her husband Jim invested more than $15,000 in three different speech therapists and a children's speech coach. While Jemma would appear to make some progress during sessions with these practitioners, all the skills she'd supposedly acquired would vanish as soon as she left the clinic. She wasn't getting enough practice and enough of the highly sensitized feedback Down's Syndrome children need to truly master speech.

4. How your solution differs from existing solutions. This part of the message plays a critical role in gaining the reader's trust. It shows that you understand the painful journey they've been traveling and are offering a genuine alternative to the paths they've tried.

To try to give Jemma more practice at home, Sharon and Jim also tried several so-called "talking tutor" applications, for both their desktop computer and their iPad. While the interactive graphics and fun sounds attracted Jemma's attention, the only benefit she seemed to take from these programs was entertainment. She'd giggle when the apps emitted words in different voices—a cat, a parakeet, a baby, and so on—but she wouldn't respond when the software asked her to take a turn.

That lack of reaction is typical. Even pre-verbal children can tell when language is being used in a natural way, as part of a genuine conversation, and when it's just being spat out at them by a computer.

> *The key to engaging children with Down's Syndrome is to make teaching interactions truly conversational.*

Jemma's trained speech therapists knew how to do that, and that's why she responded so well to them in the clinical setting. But most talking tutor software doesn't come close to mimicking real human conversation—it simply provides individual words for children to mimic.

SpeakMee overcomes this limitation by engaging children in an authentic human exchange. It uses cartoon characters to draw children into a fictional world in which they're able to interact with the characters as they would in real life. The characters run on scripts created by licensed speech therapists, so they provide just the right amount of context and support to meet the needs of children just starting to communicate through spoken language. The same characters also provide specific feedback, as part of the ongoing conversation.

5. High-level technical description. Start with an overview, focusing on what your solution does for users rather than how it does it.

Much more than a talking tutor, SpeakMee provides an immersive, true-to-life conversational experience that quickly builds confidence as well as skill.

How SpeakMee Works

SpeakMee conversation scripts are based on folktales and fairy tales familiar to young children. Knowing how the story unfolds makes it easy for them to insert themselves into the drama.

Designed by a team of certified speech therapists and speech therapy educators, SpeechMe enables parents and children to share a rich, rewarding learning experience. Besides your iPad, the only hardware you need is the SpeakMee microphone, which connects with your iPad through Bluetooth.

To begin a conversation, your child chooses a story from the main menu. A character from the story then asks for the child's name, which you type in.

Figure 3.2 (Continued)

Then the action begins. Animated characters speak with each other in short scenes of two to three sentences. At the end of each scene, a narrator figure addresses your child, inviting them to respond to simple questions with one- or two-word answers.

After your child speaks into the microphone, the narrator figure responds with appropriate feedback, providing coaching on word choice, enunciation, pitch, volume, and tone.

Figure 3.2 (Continued)

As the story unfolds, the character conversations and the narrator's questions unfold to match your child's skill level. SpeakMee adjusts the level and pace of the story scripts to focus on the particular aspects of speech your child needs to work on.

In other words, your child can snuggle up with you on your living room coach and receive the **personalized practice and feedback that** till now has been available only in a speech therapist's office.

"Gregory asks to play with SpeakMee as soon as he wakes up in the morning, and it's the last thing we do before his evening bath. The results have been transformational!"

- **Byron and Georgia Smythe, Salt City, Utah**

"In 20 years of working with Down's Syndrome children, I've never seen any take-home tool deliver such great results. You can tell the scripts have been created by expert speech therapists; the approach fits perfectly with the best practices I use in my clinic—and it really works!"

- **Aysha Koul, Registered Speech Therapist Vancouver, BC, Canada**

"Melissa has improved her speech so much through using SpeakMee. She's gained so much confidence that she has actually started making friends in her Down's Children play group."

- **Johanna Gzowski, Bangor, Maine**

Figure 3.2 (*Continued*)

| 6. Technical details. Once you've provided an overview, you may want to highlight specific technical features of your solution. Since this letter is addressed to an audience of end users, this section is brief. For an audience of advanced users or experts, you might want to expand this part of the letter, perhaps shortening the overview section. | **Playful features Both You and Your Child Will Love**

The reason SpeakMee gets such great results is that it's fun. Children enjoy the realistic feel of the interactions with the characters, and parents love the way the program adapts to individual needs.

Here are just a few of the features that earned SpeakMee the Educational Toy of the Year Award from the American Toy Council in 2018:

• 12 different stories (and new stories are added with each quarterly app update)
• 6 different narrator voices
• Lifelike 3D characters
• Customizable welcome screen (choice of colors, fonts, and background art)
• Adjustable audio speed and volume
• Optional closed captioning
• Pre-story game to make sure the software accurately recognizes the child's voice
• Bonus singalong and dance-along at the end of each story
• Recording function so you can share SpeakMee sessions with your child's speech therapist
• Optional coloring pages

SpeakMee works on the iPad Air, iPad Mini, and the iPad Pro. |
| 7. Response to anticipated objection(s). If your reader has made it all the way through a detailed description of your offering and is still reading, then they might be interested enough to make a purchase. Think back on face-to-face sales conversations you've had and the questions people have asked as they've started to think seriously about buying. Use this section of your letter to tackle one or more of those objections head-on so that your reader can base their decision on accurate information. | **But Shouldn't I Be Limiting My Child's Screen Time?**

Yes, you should certainly limit your child's passive screen time, which includes watching videos and playing games that lack educational value. Staring at a screen for hours at a time, without being mentally stimulated, has been associated with child obesity, attentional difficulties, and developmental delays in motor skills. Since Down's Syndrome children already face so many physical and cognitive challenges, it's important that any time they spend with an electronic device focus on high-value learning activities.

SpeakMee provides much more than screen entertainment. It engages a child's mind and imagination in an **active, immersive learning experience**. Through interactive dialogue with the characters, your child learns skills that will help them thrive in the real world.

That said, we recommend that you keep SpeakMee sessions to about 15 minutes since that's about how long a young child can concentrate intently on any language-building activity. We also encourage you and your child to take advantage of the opportunity the bonus singalong and dance-along content offers to get up and move. Singing and dancing to new vocabulary words will help your child remember them, and it will make your SpeakMee sessions even more fun. |

Figure 3.2 (Continued)

8. Specific offer. Clearly state what you're offering and how the reader can get it. Provide an incentive to motivate a quick decision.	**Special Early-bird Offer** SpeakMee will debut on the Apple App store starting January 15, 2020. The first 300 subscribers will receive a 15 percent discount off the regular yearly fee of $230.00 (or $22/month). Become one of these early adopters, and you'll pay **just $195.50 for the first year (or $18.70/month)**.

But wait…it gets better. **The first 100 subscribers will be entered in a draw for an all-expenses-paid family trip to Disney World** (flight, accommodations, and Disney tickets for 1 week in the Magical Kingdom, for up to five people).

To take advantage of the special early-bird rate and qualify for the draw, click the button below.

YES, SIGN ME UP FOR SPEAKMEE!

	9. Signature. To build credibility for your message, the letter should be signed by the highest-ranking person in your organization.

Best wishes to you and your family,
Mike Blatch
CEO of SpeakMee

10. P.S. Always include a P.S. as this part of the letter tends to get a lot of attention.	P.S. Daryl Johnson, chair of the Speech Therapy program at Boston University, calls SpeakMee "a game-changer for Down's Syndrome children and all who care about them." He's already pre-ordered a copy for his teaching clinic, so make sure you act on the **special early-bird offer** and get yours today!

Figure 3.2 **(Continued)**

Three Must-Haves for Building Trust through E-mail Marketing

Whether you're writing a newsletter or a sales letter, your finished messages should exhibit three must-have characteristics of persuasive marketing e-mails:

1. **Likability**. We tend to trust people we like, and we like people who seem genuine and transparent. In an e-mail, you create likability not just through the content you present but also through your writing style. Simple, straightforward sentences that sound natural and conversational make you seem a sincere, trustworthy guide.

   Try reading your e-mail marketing messages aloud. Do they sound like you? Do they convey the qualities of your brand voice you want to highlight? If not, then you may want to ask a colleague to help you refine your style to make it more likable.

2. **Reliability**. Producing a consistently likable brand voice contributes to a sense of reliability. So does sticking with a regular communication schedule and delivering uniformly high-quality content.

   If you're striving to position yourself as an expert in your field, another way to boost your reliability quotient is to show where your knowledge comes from. Incorporate into your free content data points from reputable sources, and credit those sources appropriately. Demonstrate that your knowledge has depth and substance, that it goes beyond the surface level of an infographic or fact sheet.

3. **Readability.** Shorten your paragraphs and allow generous white space. Despite what your seventh-grade English teacher may have said, one-sentence paragraphs work just fine when you're trying to emphasize an important point or ask a question.

You can also make your e-mails easy to skim by inserting headings and using bulleted lists. In addition, direct attention to important words by creating visual emphasis through techniques such as bold type, capital letters, and color. Be careful, though, not to overuse any of these, or they'll lose their effectiveness. Notice that I've not mentioned underlining; avoid that as readers may interpret underlined text as a hyperlink.

The Science of the Subject Line

As you start sending marketing e-mails, you'll want to track the opening rate. Your content may be scintillating, but no one will see it shine if they're not intrigued enough to open your message.

Crafting an attention-grabbing headline for your e-mail subject line proves to be more science than art. Professional copywriters rely on tried-and-true "formulas" for luring their audience to their content. Below are 20 of those formulas. As you read through the list, consider how you could apply each formula to the kinds of content you have to share with your e-mail list:

1. How to…
2. Do You Know How to…?
3. X Ways to…
4. X Reasons to…
5. Never [do a specific, undesirable action]
6. Do [Something] Like …
7. The Secret of…
8. What Everybody Should Know About…
9. X Lessons I Learned from…
10. Here's a Quick Way to…
11. Who Else Wants…?
12. Little Known Ways to…
13. Get Rid of [Problem] Once and for All
14. How I [achieved a specific, awe-inspiring result]…
15. Why [Option A] Beats [Option B]
16. A Brief Guide to…
17. X Common Mistakes That Prevent You from…
18. Why [doing something yields a surprising result]
19. X Time-saving [or Money-saving] Tips for…
20. Have a [desired outcome] You Can Be Proud of…

I've left the subject line till last because many people find it easiest and most effective to craft the headline after they've written the body of their e-mail. I encourage you to brainstorm multiple subject lines (at least 6 to 10) for each marketing e-mail you create and then choose the option you think will resonate most strongly with your readers. As you become more proficient at e-mail marketing, you may want to do split A/B testing of your subject lines. That involves dividing your e-mail list in two and sending the same message with two different subject lines so you can gather hard data about what appeals to your audience.

For help generating subject lines—and for tips regarding content marketing in general—I recommend copyblogger.com. Founder Brian Clark was one of the pioneers of copywriting, and he and his team provide in-depth insights to help both rookies and experienced writers fine-tune their skills.

You'll also find online a number of automated tools that supposedly analyze the effectiveness of a headline, such as CoSchedule's headline analyzer. Not being an AI expert, I can't comment on their usefulness. I can say, though, that generally speaking, your readers will give you the best feedback. Discipline yourself to listen to them—to track and analyze the results of your e-mail messages—and you will become the true expert on your audience and their preferences.

Checklist for E-mail Newsletters

❑ Branded template
❑ Attractive, spacious layout, including at least one visual
❑ Compliance with applicable e-mail regulations (e.g., CASL, CAN-SPAM, GDPR)
❑ Attention-grabbing subject line
❑ Intriguing first paragraph that shows why the e-mail is worth reading
❑ High-value content readers can put to practical use
❑ Conversational tone
❑ Clear call to action

Checklist for E-mail Sales Letters

❑ Attention-grabbing subject line
❑ Personalized greeting
❑ Internal headline
❑ Story illustrating the problem your solution solves
❑ Testimonials
❑ How your solution differs from existing solutions
❑ High-level technical description
❑ Technical details
❑ Response to anticipated objection(s)
❑ Specific offer
❑ Signature
❑ P.S.

CHAPTER 4

Web Writing

Trying to attract an Internet user's interest is like trying to catch a buzzing insect in your bare hands. The average website visitor spends just 10 to 20 seconds[1] on a page, so your web copy must be "sticky." Like flypaper, it must stop site visitors in their tracks and convince them to stay around long enough to skim through your headings and, if you're really lucky, scroll past the first chunk of content.

Because web visitors have gnat-sized attention spans, writing for the web is like practicing an extreme sport. It challenges you to achieve levels of clarity and conciseness beyond what paper-based documents or e-mails require.

To succeed at web writing, you need to get 100 percent clear on who your audience is, why they're visiting your site, and what you have to offer them. You also need a laser-sharp focus on usability. Website visitors don't just passively absorb your content; they interact with it as "users." We'll focus intently on users throughout this chapter, as we explore some ways you can connect with your particular user group, attract and keep their interest, and persuade them to engage with you beyond your website.

How to Get Intimate with a Mass Audience

When you write an e-mail message, you're addressing one or more specific readers. Even if you've never met them, you can identify them as individuals and, as we saw in Chapter 1, conduct various kinds of research to get a sense of their needs, values, interests, biases, and so on. When

---

[1] J. Nielsen. September 11, 2011. "How Long Do Users Stay on Web Pages?" *Nielsen Norman Group website*. https://www.nngroup.com/articles/how-long-do-users-stay-on-web-pages/.

you're writing for a website, on the other hand, you're writing for a mass audience. Like the host of a TV show, a radio show, or a podcast, you're broadcasting your message to a wide variety of people, most of whom you'll never be able to identify individually.

But here's the rub: each user who arrives at your site must feel as if the content has been crafted specifically for them. "The masses" have no patience for web writing that speaks to them as if they're a mass. They'll take the time to read your copy only if it resonates with them at a deeply personal level.

If you craft your web copy as if it's written for everyone, it will engage no one. So the key is to write for a handful of representative "someones" in your target audience. You can do that by developing a set of detailed avatars[2] representing your audience.

An avatar is an imaginary, composite character you invent so you can picture how real users will interact with your website. Creating avatars and designing your web content for them helps you avoid two common pitfalls of writing for a mass audience:

1. Thinking too narrowly, in terms of how a handful of actual clients would react to your writing (limiting your audience analysis to "How would Jim interpret that?" or "I don't think Sharon would like that")
2. Thinking of users in terms of just their information needs, without taking into account their psychological and emotional reality and the circumstances surrounding their interaction with your writing

Christine Ward-Paige is a scientist-founder who has worked extensively with avatars to shape the website for her company eOceans, which

[2]Market researchers use the term "persona" instead of "avatar," but I prefer to use "persona" to refer to the voice and image the writer creates for themselves (as described in Chapter 2). This usage connects more directly to the origin of the term, which comes from the theater of Ancient Greece. In that context, the "persona" was the mask performers wore to amplify their voice.

Using "avatar" to describe web users helps us remember that when we're writing for the web, we're writing in an interactive context. Just as avatars in a video game make different choices and perform different tasks, so do users engaging with a website's content.

addresses a remarkably diverse group of users. Christine's user base spans the globe, multiple industries, and a range of demographic groups because she's in the business of crowdsourcing data. The eOceans crowdsourcing platform collects data about ocean life from a wide variety of sources, including scientists, government agencies, and people who make their living from the sea, such as fishers and owners of dive shops. The platform also shares data with these different groups, providing them with real-time information they can use in their various contexts.

Christine turned to avatars to help develop her web copy because no single or composite profile could possibly capture the different characteristics and needs of people who visit the eOceans website (https://www. eoceans.co/). For instance, some eOceans users have a PhD, while others have little formal education. Some speak English, but a number of languages are also represented in the user group. (Many eOceans clients are based in Indonesia, Thailand, and Fiji.) Additionally, Christine's users access her site through different kinds of devices. They might visit the site from a desktop in a university office, a laptop on a research vessel, or a mobile phone on a dock.

Before she started to craft her web copy, Christine recognized that she faced a dilemma: How could she possibly write for such a variety of clients and colleagues without alienating some of them? As a good scientist, she took a scientific approach to the problem, using avatars.

Christine reckoned her audience comprised about 40 different types of people, so she created a detailed avatar for each type. She gave each avatar a well-rounded profile that included such information as their geographical location level of education, level of literacy, native language, age, gender, occupation, and, most importantly, their reason for contributing to and accessing data about ocean life. She entered all this avatar data into a spreadsheet so she could highlight common themes and look for commonalities.

What on earth, you might ask, would someone running a diving operation for tourists from a small town in Fiji have in common with a government-funded researcher working in the Arctic? Christine's detailed analysis of her avatars showed her that three needs unite everyone in her audience: the need for speed, the need for accuracy, and the need for detailed information that's not currently available.

Members of the eOceans audience fall into four broad categories:

1. Those who study the oceans (scientists and student-scientists)
2. Those who make their living from the oceans (fishers, divers, owners of dive shops)
3. Those who manage the oceans (government researchers, policymakers, and legislators)
4. Those who use the ocean recreationally (a broad spectrum of users, from tourists to people who use the ocean daily for social and cultural reasons)

A common frustration among all groups is the amount of time it traditionally takes for scientific data about ocean life to get collected and distributed. All three groups need to make decisions and take actions based on that data. The closer they can get to accessing it in real time, the better they can judge and advise on emerging situations.

With the common "need for speed" in mind, Christine's ongoing challenge is to enable her 40 different kinds of users to quickly and easily find content to help them with the decisions and actions they want to take. Whether your audience avatars number in the dozens or you can count them on one hand, as is more often the case, this is the essential dilemma that confronts anyone writing web copy.

Fortunately, once you frame the problem correctly, you're more than halfway to finding the solution. The key is to consider your web users as *hunters seeking information to support specific goals.* It's also important to empathize with your users' emotional state. *What kinds of feelings do they bring with them as they come to your site looking for help?* When you write for web users with their goals and emotions in mind, the experience of interacting with your site feels personalized and meaningful to them, even if your customers or clients form a group as diverse as Christine's.

Let's take Christine's three broad audience groups as examples to investigate. As we start thinking through content for each group, the first question that comes to mind might be "What does this group need to know?" But that question casts web users in a passive role, as if they're empty vessels just waiting for us to pour information into them. If we understand them more properly as information hunters on a mission, then our starting point becomes "What does each group want to do?" Table 4.1 shows how changing the line of questioning gives us more specific insight into how to create and organize content tailored to each audience group:

Table 4.1 Assessment of web user needs

Audience group	What do they need to know?	What do they want to do?	What emotions are they feeling?
People who study the oceans (scientists and student-scientists)	• Number of specific marine species (by species, region, and worldwide) • Change in local and global trends concerning growth or decline of specific species • Environmental data relevant to such topics as plastics, invasive species, or climate change	• Decide what to study • Compare data from other studies with data from their current study • Relate global trends to specific trends and topics they're researching	• Frustrated by the difficulty of finding up-to-date, comprehensive data related to their field of study • Excited about the possibility of accessing real-time data • Passionate about finding and using reliable data to solve complex, urgent problems • Ambitious about elevating their reputation as a researcher • Eager to make their research more collaborative and accessible
People who make their living from the oceans (fishers, divers, owners of dive shops)	• Number of specific marine species in local area • Trends impacting growth or decline of species in local area	• Decide what species to fish or to feature in diving tours • Assess the viability of fishing or offering diving tours • Predict how external trends will impact their business or livelihood • Mitigate issues that may impact their business	• Anxious about not knowing what kind of season they'll have this year • Worried about revenue and the long-term sustainability of their business • Yearning for a predictable, secure livelihood
People who manage the oceans (government researchers, legislators, policy makers)	• Number of specific marine species (by species, region, and worldwide) • Changes in local and global trends concerning growth or decline of specific species • Data regarding climate change and other factors driving change in the oceans	• Access data to support or contradict proposed policies and legislation • Access data to incorporate in government reports • Decide which research initiatives to fund	• Frustrated by not having the data they need to drive or support policy changes • Challenged by need to present data in ways non-experts can easily understand • Confused about how to choose among competing research priorities • Keen to make research results more accessible and to increase stakeholder buy-in to decisions

As you can see, information needs don't differ significantly among the three groups; people in all three categories want access to data about the growth and decline of specific marine species as well as insights into trends related to that topic. But the three groups vary distinctly in the goals they want to achieve and in the emotions they're experiencing related to their situation. These differences shape the expectations they bring to the website and their experience interacting with it.

To make it easy for avatars with a more pragmatic focus to quickly access her web content, Christine has created small infographics on specific topics, such as the number of sharks killed every year. Depending on the depth of knowledge they need, users can simply view the infographic, or they can follow a link to read the scientific paper the graphic summarizes. While complex visuals can sometimes create challenges for mobile users, Christine designs all her infographics with mobile in mind so that the group of "people who make their living from the oceans" can easily access data without needing a laptop or desktop computer.

I strongly recommend Christine's method of creating avatars because writing copy that resonates with the different people in your audience requires that you intentionally see them as individuals. If this seems a daunting task, keep in mind that the eOceans audience is particularly diverse; in most cases, three to five avatars will adequately represent the range of a site's anticipated users.

As you create avatars, here are a few guiding principles to keep in mind:

- **An avatar should *not* represent a real client.** Avatars work best when they're creative composites, including qualities you'd find in several different clients. If you base your content design on the specific profiles of real clients, your focus will be too narrow.
- **An avatar profile should include psychographic as well as demographic information (attitudes, beliefs, and values).** As we saw when analyzing individual readers in Chapter 1, in many cases the psychographic information provides more valuable insights than does the demographic data.
- **Focus on the avatar's personal mission.** Why have they come to your website? What challenge do they need help addressing? What do they hope to do with the information they find?
- **Remember the emotions.** An avatar without emotions represents a robot, not a human being. And human beings are largely driven

by emotion, even when making consequential decisions you'd think would be based mainly on logic and reason. (Think that doesn't describe you or your users? Check out Daniel Kahneman's book *Thinking, Fast and Slow* for some shocking insights into we really make choices, even when we believe we're being objective and strategic.)

The specific attributes you include in your avatar profiles will depend on your user group and your business. Here's an example of an avatar for the eOceans site (Figure 4.1):

Jana Dahl

Age: 34

Education: PhD in Marine Science from the University of Australia

Occupation: Lead Researcher, Ocean Renewal Study

Location: Stockholm, Sweden (University of Stockholm)

Research interests: Effects of increased ocean acidity on bottom-feeding fish

Research challenges:
- Lack of funding to gather her own data
- Age of data by the time it's accessible through academic journals
- Difficulty comparing data from different parts of the world
- Lack of data related specifically to bottom-feeding fish in Australasia

Group affiliations:
- Global Coalition of Scientists Against Climate Change
- Swedish Society of Female Divers
- Editorial Board for *Journal of Ocean Research*

What gets her out of bed in the morning:
- Passion to help heal the oceans
- Relentless drive for discovery
- Desire to make her mark as a leading researcher in her field

What keeps her up at night:
- Anxiety about climate change
- Upcoming meeting with tenure committee
- Cuts to travel funding for research
- Stress of juggling teaching, research, and personal life (hard to find quality time to spend with her partner, David)

Figure 4.1 Sample avatar profile

Writing for the Insect Brain

Creating avatars for your website will help you decide what you need to write and how to organize it for your goal-oriented users. The next step is to consider how you'll express it. Web writing requires an ultra-lean style that breaks down ideas and information into the smallest, most visually enticing bits we can create.

In one of Franz Kafka's most famous stories,[3] a man wakes up one day to discover he has become a beetle. That, to my mind, is what happens to "readers" when they become "web users." It's as if our mammalian attention span and processing abilities suddenly shrink to beetle-size. This Kafkaesque "metamorphosis" explains why trying to repurpose a traditional document, such as a report or white paper, as online content never works.

To connect with your audience online, you need to adopt a style that appeals to the insect brain. Fortunately, mastering beetle-speak is easier than you might think. Use these four simple principles as your guide, and you'll be well on your way:

1. **Practice "letting go of the words."** This principle comes from web usability expert Ginny Redish, whose 2012 book on web writing is as relevant today as it was when Web 2.0 was just emerging.

   Letting Go of the Words: Writing Web Content That Works operates on the assumption that web users don't "read" in the traditional sense. Instead, they forage for specific pieces of information and then dip in and out pieces of content that attract their momentary attention. Given these unreaderly habits, we must burden them with as little reading material as possible.

   This means abandoning conventional paragraphs and sentences as primary units of meaning. The aim is to communicate meaning in as few pixels as possible, using headings, micro-paragraphs, and lists as ways to hold ideas and information together:

   • **Headings** enable users to preview a webpage's content as they rapidly skim it, hunting for words and phrases relevant to them.

---

[3] F. Kafka. *The Metamorphosis*, trans. D. Wyllie (Project Gutenberg). http://www.gutenberg.org/files/5200/5200-h/5200-h.htm, (accessed September 28, 2019).

The most effective headings are both concise and descriptive. Avoid generic headings and opt instead for precise headings that sum up the key message of the section that follows. Rather than "Benefits of a Zipline Installation," you might try "A Full Aerobic Workout in Your Own Backyard" or "Three Reasons Fitness Trainers Recommend Zipline."

- **Micro-paragraphs** present content in the visual equivalent of soundbites. On paper, a typical paragraph runs to five or seven sentences, but on the web, three to four sentences or so should be your limit. One- or two-sentence paragraphs allow you to emphasize key ideas by surrounding them with white space.

- **Lists** create packets of content that are easy to skim and remember. Keep the number of items to seven or less, and reserve numbered lists for sequenced steps or items presented in a priority sequence.

    List items must belong to the same category, or their structure loses its logic. For instance, you might create a list of examples, benefits, features, or reasons to justify a point. But you wouldn't use a list to create an argument. For that, you need a paragraph of logically linked sentences to show the development of your ideas.

To Engage Your Users, Serve Them a Layer-cake

Eye-tracking technology has enabled researchers to identify users' scanning patterns as they interact with web pages. Back in 2006, an often-cited study showed that many users scan a web page in an F-pattern.[1] They start with a horizontal scan across the top of the page, jump further down the page and do another horizontal scan, and then do a quick vertical scan down the left side of the screen. This approach differs from the Z-shaped pattern readers tend to follow when processing paper-based documents.

---

[1] J. Nielsen. April 16, 2006. "F-shaped Pattern for Reading Web Content (Original Study)," *Nielsen Norman Group website.* https://www.nngroup.com/articles/f-shaped-pattern-reading-web-content-discovered/, (accessed September 30, 2019).

It's also an approach that can cause users to miss important information on a web page. As you lay out your content, think about how to guide the user's eye so they can quickly access information they're hunting for without missing important content you want them to see. One of the most effective ways to do this is to create a series of headings and subheadings that encourages a "layer-cake scanning pattern."[2] When you divide your content into small sections, grouped under subheadings, users tend to scan from heading to heading, pausing occasionally on the small chunks of text in between. This makes scanning efficient and rewarding for them, and they're likely to at least glance at the main points you want to communicate to them.

You can also guide the way users scan your web page by strategically placing your graphic elements, such as visuals, enlarged text, and bold type. The key principle to keep in mind is to lay out your content so the user can identify and access the information that interests them by exerting the least effort possible.

---

[2]K. Pernice. August 4, 2019. "The Layer-cake Pattern of Scanning Content on the Web," *Nielsen Norman Group website*. https://www.nngroup.com/articles/layer-cake-pattern-scanning/, (accessed September 30, 2019).

2. **Avoid distracting "padding."** Convey the essence of your ideas and information, with as little "padding" around it as possible. Here are 10 kinds of padding to prune from your sentences, headings, and lists:
   1. Multisyllable words (unless these are absolutely required for technical accuracy)
   2. Passive verbs[4]
   3. Weak verbs (such as *to be* and *to have*)
   4. Noun forms of verbs (e.g., replace *perform the installation* with *install*)
   5. Unnecessary prefaces (e.g., *It is recommended that, We believe that, In our professional opinion*)

---

[4]A passive verb presents the subject as receiving rather than performing an action, e.g., "When the lever *is pressed* by the operator, the system *is stopped*." To rewrite a passive verb using an active verb, make sure the subject of the sentence acts as the agent doing the action, e.g., "When *the operator presses* the lever, the *system stops*."

6. Unneeded adjectives and adverbs (e.g., *We appreciate your ~~valuable~~ contribution, We have ~~successfully~~ completed six projects in Indonesia)*

7. Meaningless descriptors (e.g., *very, quite, somewhat, sizable*)

8. Redundancies (e.g., *mutual consensus, the color red, total catastrophe*)

9. Verbal throat-clearings (e.g., *We would like to announce…, Welcome to the site of Company X!, For those of you who are unfamiliar with our product line…*)

10. Old-fashioned phrases (e.g., *henceforth, suffice it to say*)

3. **Adopt a conversational tone.** Depending on your company brand, conversational does not necessarily mean casual. Consider the way you present yourself when you speak with a client over the phone or in a face-to-face meeting. That's the way you'll want to present yourself online so that your organization comes across as energetic, likable, and trustworthy.

   If you've spent career time in an academic or public-sector context, adopting a conversational style could prove challenging for you. Both academic writing and bureaucratic writing encourage a formal, impersonal style (along with bloated sentences and long paragraphs). What impresses journal editors, however, quickly frustrates web users (even if those web users also read journal articles). Online, a more down-to-earth, everyday style will attract and keep your users' attention.

   Here's a quick test to find out how conversationally you're communicating online: Try reading your web copy aloud. If it doesn't roll off your tongue easily or sound natural to your ear, then you've got a problem. Try swapping out some of your formal language and elaborate sentence structures for more everyday phrasing.

4. **Communicate visually.** Although I've encouraged you to create sound-bites and test your writing with your ear, remember that your overall aim should be to "let go of the words." But that doesn't mean avoiding or dumbing down the complex, innovative ideas you have to share. Rather, it means inventing creative visual ways to communicate those ideas, through charts, tables, conceptual diagrams, and infographics:

   • **Tables** enable users to compare and contrast information at a glance. They work particularly well when you want to show present and future states, pros and cons, or a range of product options.

- **Charts** provide "hard" evidence to support claims about your product or service. Make sure you label them clearly (provide a title as well as labels for each axis) and guide user interpretation. (Provide a summary of the data as a way of introducing the chart.)
- **Conceptual diagrams** give users a mental framework for processing a complex idea. For example, a pyramid can show how development phases start with a foundational stage and then build upon each other, and a cycle diagram can make a complex process easy to grasp. If you're new to conveying concepts through diagrams, PowerPoint's SmartArt feature provides ready-made templates for common kinds of concepts.
- **Infographics** shape various data points into a visual storyline that grabs attention and is easy to remember. You can create simple infographics using PowerPoint, which now includes a starter icon set. More and more free infographic templates and generators are also cropping up online, such as Piktochart and Visme.

Figure 4.2 shows how applying the four principles of web writing transforms a hard-copy document into something new, suitable to the "insect brain" of online readers.

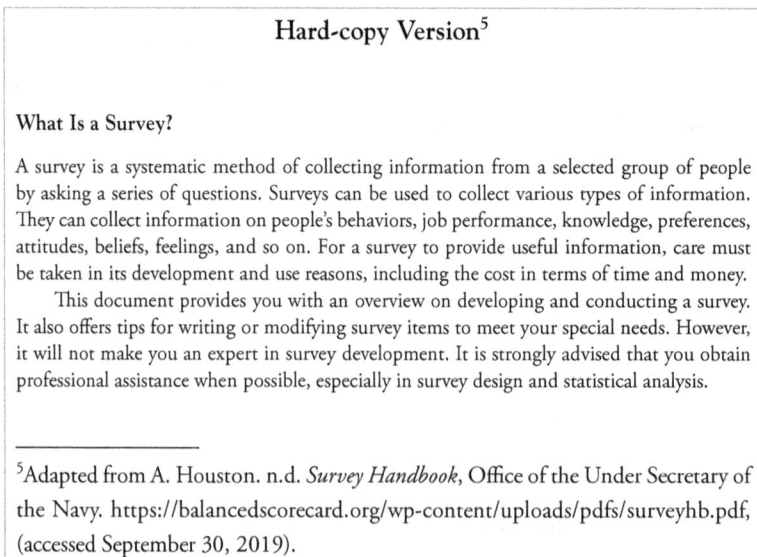

Hard-copy Version[5]

What Is a Survey?

A survey is a systematic method of collecting information from a selected group of people by asking a series of questions. Surveys can be used to collect various types of information. They can collect information on people's behaviors, job performance, knowledge, preferences, attitudes, beliefs, feelings, and so on. For a survey to provide useful information, care must be taken in its development and use reasons, including the cost in terms of time and money.

This document provides you with an overview on developing and conducting a survey. It also offers tips for writing or modifying survey items to meet your special needs. However, it will not make you an expert in survey development. It is strongly advised that you obtain professional assistance when possible, especially in survey design and statistical analysis.

---

[5]Adapted from A. Houston. n.d. *Survey Handbook*, Office of the Under Secretary of the Navy. https://balancedscorecard.org/wp-content/uploads/pdfs/surveyhb.pdf, (accessed September 30, 2019).

Figure 4.2 Hard-copy document rewritten for the web

When Should I Use a Survey?

Although surveys are a popular method of collecting data, they must be used under the appropriate conditions. Consider using a survey when it is faster, easier, or less expensive to use than other methods. Sometimes other data collection methods are preferable. For example, to determine the number of people using a clinic, you can simply count the number of signatures on the sign-in sheet, or examine the daily records, rather than conducting a survey to obtain this information. Also consider the use of a survey when the information does not already exist in some form. Checking whether relevant and accurate data exist in archives, records, or databases can save a great deal of time, money, and effort. For example, before asking employees the names and dates of each course taken within the past year, consult their training files to obtain this information.

Preparing for a Survey

A number of issues should be resolved before drafting the first survey item. Use the following questions to help you in preparing for a survey:

What Is the Purpose of the Survey?
Surveys can be used for many purposes, including:

- Determining customer needs/assessing customer satisfaction
- Testing messaging
- Identifying organizational strengths and weaknesses
- Targeting areas needing improvement
- Assessing the effectiveness of new or existing policies or programs

Without a clear purpose, it is likely that the survey effort will flounder. This can result in wasted resources, useless data, and disappointment on the part of those who initiated the survey and those who responded to it.

Who Will Use the Results?
Identify who will be using the results of the survey and what their information needs are. What types of decisions are they going to make based on the results? How should the information be sorted for them? Do they need detailed responses or is the "big picture" sufficient? How do they prefer to have information presented to them?

What Specific Information Is Needed?
To meet the purpose of the survey, identify the topics or issues of interest and the forms of information needed. For example, if you are interested in maintaining equipment at an athletic center, then you might ask questions about how often people use the center, what facilities they use, and hours of use. You might also ask people to rate the quality of the swimming pool, treadmills, exercise machines, shower area, towel service, and so on. If you are interested in meeting future needs, you might ask people to identify their anticipated physical fitness needs or interests. Each of these topics could be the subject of one or more survey items.

Web Version

What Is a Survey?

A survey is a systematic method of collecting information from a selected group of people by asking a series of questions.

With SurveyMaker, you can easily design simple surveys. If the question you're investigating is complex, we recommend you engage a professional researcher to help you create and conduct the survey.

> Notice the use of "you" throughout the web copy. Addressing the reader directly makes your style conversational and engaging.

> Microparagraphs make it easy for users to skim the content.

> Since a caution such as this is important, it's placed near the beginning of the web copy.

Figure 4.2 (Continued)

What Kind of Information Can I Collect Through a Survey?

You can use a survey to collect various types of information, including qualitative data as well as quantitative data. Here are some examples of information Survey-Maker clients have collected:

- Job performance data
- Customer retention data
- Brand preferences
- Attitudes toward a topic in the news
- Beliefs related to brand quality
- Feelings associated with a particular problem

When Should I Use a Survey?

A survey is your best bet when:
- Other methods would be slower, more difficult, or more expensive to use

  and
- The information you want doesn't already exist. (Check your organization's records, archives, and databases to make sure you're not duplicating effort.)

Preparing for a Survey

Before you start creating your survey in SurveyMaker, take a few minutes to consider these mission-critical questions:

	Helpful Hints
What is the purpose of the survey?	Some common purposes include: • Determine customer needs/assessing customer satisfaction • Identify organizational strengths and weaknesses • Target areas needing improvement • Assess the effectiveness of new or existing policies or programs Make sure you get clear on *your* particular purpose. Otherwise, you'll risk wasting time and effort creating a survey that doesn't deliver the results you wanted.
Who will use the results?	Some questions to ask about the people who will be using the survey data: • What types of decisions are they going to make based on the results? • Do they need detailed responses or is the "big picture" sufficient? • How do they prefer to have information presented to them?
What specific information is needed?	Identify the topics or issues of interest and the forms of information needed. For example, if you are interested in maintaining equipment at an athletic center, then you might ask questions about how often people use the center, what facilities they use, and hours of use. You might also ask people to rate the quality of the swimming pool, treadmills, exercise machines, shower area, towel service, and so on.

Side annotations:
- Increasing the number of headings makes the content easier to scan.
- Examples have been made more specific so it's easier for the target audience to relate to them.
- A bulleted list makes skimming easier and also highlights the examples.
- Original text has been abbreviated because less is more when you're writing for web users.
- Contractions also help create a conversational style.
- Informal language makes your tone feel more personal. Just make sure you don't cross over the line into slang that would either be inappropriate for a professional setting or unfamiliar to some of your readers.
- Using a table to present the preparation questions draws attention to this key content, particularly for users who need in-depth help with survey design. The dual-column layout also makes it easy for advanced users to skim the general questions without getting slowed down by details.

Figure 4.2 (Continued)

Keep Your Eye on the Engagement Prize

By now, you understand that web users don't want information for information's sake. They land on your home page with specific goals they want to achieve, and your job is to create copy that makes it as easy as possible for them to achieve those goals.

And then what? Once you've created "sticky" pages that attract users and helped them access the information they're looking for, how do you capitalize on their interest in what you have to offer?

To answer that question, you must be clear about your goals. How do you want to continue to engage with the people who've visited your website? What specific step do you want them to take so that you can open a communication channel with them?

Every web page you write is a sales page. If you're not selling your products or services, you're selling your credibility and trustworthiness as an organization. After someone visits your website, then, their next step should lead them into your sales process. This means that each page you create should include some kind of a call to action, a clear direction to engage further with you.

A call to action doesn't need to be pushy. Think of it as an invitation to start a conversation with you. For instance, you might invite web users to take one of the following steps:

- Call you for more information.
- Download a one-pager describing your offerings (see Chapter 10 for help creating such a document).
- Check out a sales page on your website.
- Sign up for your newsletter.
- Download a free resource, such as a report or eBook (see the next chapter for help creating one of these website give-aways).
- Book a free consultation with you.
- Schedule a product demo.

If you write super-sticky web copy following all the principles in this chapter but don't include calls to action in it, then all your hard work may yield little result. Capturing your audience's flitting attention is only a start. It's how you direct that attention that turns web users into prospects and prospects into leads, potential customers or clients.

A great way to begin that conversion process is to craft a free resource you can offer on your website in exchange for a user's e-mail address. In the next chapter, you'll discover how to get started creating web give-aways that will entice your particular target audience to sign up for your e-mail list so you can keep engaging with them on a regular basis.

Checklist for Web Writing

- ❏ Clearly defined avatars for the website (at least three)
- ❏ Avatar descriptions include:
  - ○ Avatar's mission (reason for visiting the website)
  - ○ Information the avatar is seeking
  - ○ Psychographic as well as demographic information about the avatar
  - ○ Emotions the avatar is feeling (with regard to their reason for visiting the website)
- ❏ Content laid out for easy skimming:
  - ○ Short sections
  - ○ Headings and subheadings (to encourage a layer-cake scanning pattern)
  - ○ Micro-paragraphs
  - ○ Lists
- ❏ Lean style, without "padding", such as:
  - ○ Multisyllable words (unless these are absolutely required for technical accuracy)
  - ○ Passive verbs
  - ○ Weak verbs (such as *to be* and *to have*)
  - ○ Noun forms of verbs (e.g., replace *perform the installation* with *install*)
  - ○ Unnecessary prefaces (e.g., *It is recommended that, We believe that, In our professional opinion*)
  - ○ Unneeded adjectives and adverbs (e.g., *We appreciate your valuable contribution, We have successfully completed six projects in Indonesia*)
  - ○ Meaningless descriptors (e.g., *very, quite, somewhat, sizable*)
  - ○ Redundancies (e.g., *mutual consensus, the color red, total catastrophe*)
  - ○ Verbal throat-clearings (e.g., *We would like to announce…, Welcome to the site of Company X!, For those of you who are unfamiliar with our product line…*)
  - ○ Old-fashioned phrases (e.g., *henceforth, suffice it to say*)

❑ Conversational tone that:
  ○ Addresses the reader as "you"
  ○ Uses contractions
  ○ Includes colloquial language and expressions
❑ Visual communication through such graphical elements as:
  ○ Tables
  ○ Charts
  ○ Conceptual diagrams
  ○ Infographics
❑ Clear, direct call to action

CHAPTER 5

Website Giveaways

If you read just one book on marketing this year, make it Seth Godin's *This Is Marketing*. Seth gets what marketing means for those of us who are in business because we want to make change happen. Marketing, he says, is how you go about "sharing your path to better."[1]

For the people in your target market, a free giveaway from your website provides a first step along that path. Sometimes called "lead magnets," such documents also create great opportunities to rev up your marketing. Each time you add a new free download to your website, you can advertise it widely to your audience via e-mail, social media, your newsletter, and other channels.

In case you're worried that sharing free knowledge and advice could undermine your ability to get paid for your products and services, let's lay that fear to rest right now. Giving away valuable free information enhances your brand image in multiple ways:

- Creating authoritative content positions you as expert in your field.
- Offering that content for free associates you with generosity, a quality that fosters goodwill.
- Proactively serving your audience shows you have their interests at heart and deserve their trust.

Website giveaways come in many different forms. Your first step will be to decide which topic and form will best serve your audience and boost your brand image. Then, as you create your free content, you'll want to think about how to create a strong emotional connection with

---

[1]S. Godin. 2018. *This Is Marketing* (New York, NY: Portfolio/Penguin), p. xvi, Kindle.

your audience, fine-tune your writing style and visual design, and entice potential customers to take the next step along the path to better.

Choosing the Topic and Form

To quote Seth again, "Marketing is the generous act of helping someone solve a problem. Their problem."[2] A website giveaway allows you to show your target audience how clearly you understand their particular problem and how zealous you are to help them solve it.

As you brainstorm possible topics for your giveaway, you may want to create a sticky note reminder with these words on it: "Offering free help is NOT selling." To earn the goodwill and trust of your target audience, the information and advice you give away must constitute a real gift, not a disguised sales pitch. If you want to present yourself as a disinterested guide, then you must maintain that attitude throughout your giveaway. Your closing call to action should invite your audience to engage in a deeper conversation with you about your products or services—but up until that point, stay true to your mission of providing the most focused, genuinely helpful content you can create.

Your ideal topic should target a narrowly defined problem, either a small problem that causes your audience great irritation or a particular aspect of a large problem. A tight focus allows you to deliver precise insights your audience can immediately apply. Think practical tips, not context or theory. The more laser-focused your topic, the easier you make it for your audience to experience positive results right away. Those results then generate trust in your brand and your offerings, encouraging prospects to explore other, more consequential ways you could help them with broader, tougher problems.

Here are some questions to reflect on as you consider possible topics for your web giveaway:

- What problem do your customers complain about most often?
- What small problem causes big frustration?

---

[2]Godin, *This Is Marketing*, p. 2, Kindle.

- What small problem is the tip of the iceberg (evidence of much larger, unrecognized problem)?
- What questions do they most often ask?
- What top-of-mind problem could you solve for a customer in a 10-minute conversation?

Once you've picked your topic, it's time to decide on the form your giveaway will take. Here are a few possibilities to consider:

- Report
- How-to guide
- Checklist
- Training video
- Mini course
- Series of podcast episodes
- List article
- FAQ article
- Infographic

Increasingly, organizations are making their free downloads media-rich (e.g., a free e-course, podcast episode, or video). Whatever format your giveaway takes, your essential task remains the same: to provide valuable content in a way that builds emotional resonance and leads your audience to the next step in engaging with you and your sales process.

Creating Emotional Resonance

Emotional resonance happens when you tune in closely to the emotional reality of your target audience. When you express the feelings, innermost thoughts, and values that shape your audience's inner world, they reverberate with the sentiments you share. Your language "strikes a chord" with them, and the resulting sense of harmony creates a deep connection with you and your brand.

Emotional resonance plays a critical role in building positive rapport with your audience. Even if the free content you're sharing concentrates on technical information, make sure you connect the technical to the emotional. By doing that, you'll come across as a helpful, caring guide people can admire, believe, and trust. On the other hand, if you stick just to "the facts," you'll run the risk of seeming impersonal, uncaring, and pedantic.

To create a sense of emotional sync with your audience, consider three aspects of their situation with regard to the topic you're explaining:

- **Current state**—What emotions are they experiencing in their current state as a result of their unsolved problem? Common examples include fear, anxiety, worry, distress, confusion, as well as the longing for freedom from such negative feelings.
- **Future state**—How would they like to feel? How will they feel once their problem has been solved? Some examples of positive emotions associated with the "problem solved" state include relief, happiness, security, peace, and confidence.
- **Ease of implementation**—How will they feel while solving the problem in the way you're suggesting? Consider ways to emphasize how simple, easy, and straightforward your solution is.

Fine-Tuning Writing Tone and Visual Design

Together, your writing tone and visual design help create emotional resonance and convey the strengths of your brand.

1. Writing Tone

Tone is the attitude you take toward your audience, and it will depend on the kind of role you construct for yourself as the expert behind the giveaway. What kind of helper do you want to position yourself as? A scientific expert? An academic authority? A friendly teacher? A peer mentor? A kindly professor? A trusted adviser?

Different helper profiles will resonate with different audiences, depending on their occupation, industry, and life experience. Be sure, therefore, to construct a writing personality that fits with who you are and also implies the kind of authority figure your audience instinctively trusts.

The tone of your giveaway will also result from particular choices you make about word usage and phrasing. Consider how a typical person in your helper role conducts themselves in a professional conversation:

- Do they use formal or casual language?
- Do they use contractions?
- What kind of slang (if any) do they use? How about jargon or shop talk?
- What style of humor do they favor?

2. Visual Design

The visual design of your giveaway reinforces the tone created through your text. When well-executed, it can also intensify emotional resonance.

For starters, make sure the visual design of your web giveaway aligns with the basic elements of your brand, such as colors and fonts. If you can afford it, you may want to hire a graphic designer to lay out your content professionally, inserting such attention-grabbing features as sidebars, enlarged quotes, and conceptual diagrams, maybe even an infographic. Aim for the kind of creativity and finesse you'd find in a magazine. Strong visual design provides an elegant showcase for your content, making it seem more credible and trustworthy.

Your visual style choices should align with the style choices that shape your written content. If you're presenting yourself as a laid-back peer mentor, the visual design of your giveaway should signal friendly, lighthearted energy. In contrast, if you're positioning yourself as a trusted business adviser, then your design should create a more serious, corporate look-and-feel.

But don't let the challenge of creating an alluring visual design prevent you from getting your web giveaway to your market quickly. As we'll see in the chapter on one-pagers, you don't necessarily need a graphic designer to create polished electronic documents. With just a splash of color and one or two graphic elements—such as a focus box, side bar, or image—you can amp up visual appeal without stretching your budget. For example, Figure 5.1 shows a page from one of my website giveaways, an e-book called *Clarity Without Compromise: How to Truly Connect with the People Reading Your Technical and Scientific Documents*.

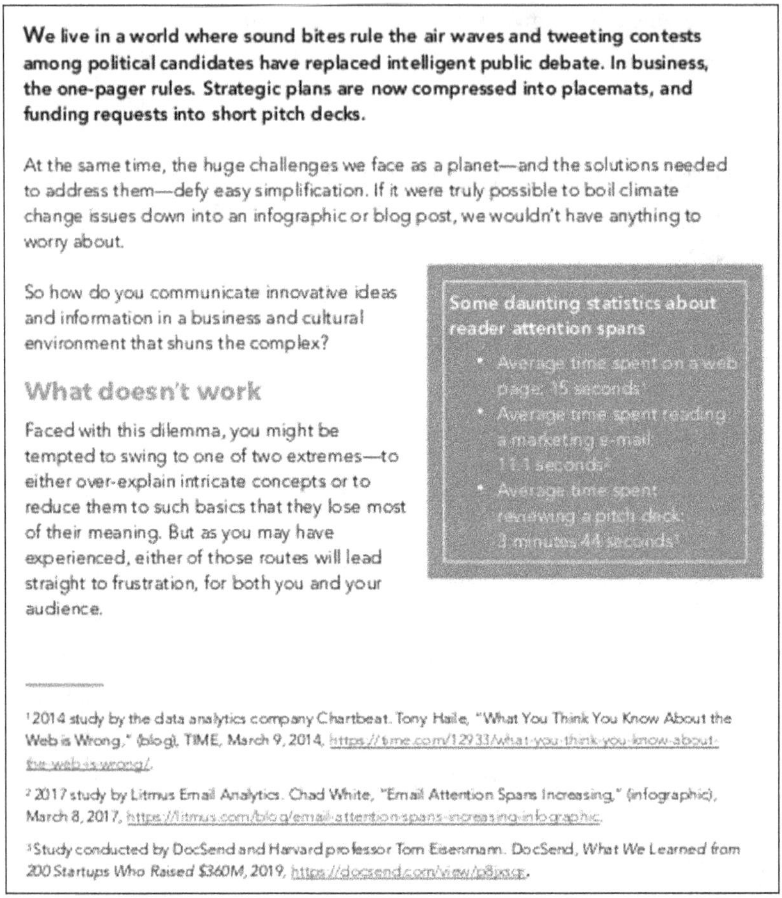

We live in a world where sound bites rule the air waves and tweeting contests among political candidates have replaced intelligent public debate. In business, the one-pager rules. Strategic plans are now compressed into placemats, and funding requests into short pitch decks.

At the same time, the huge challenges we face as a planet—and the solutions needed to address them—defy easy simplification. If it were truly possible to boil climate change issues down into an infographic or blog post, we wouldn't have anything to worry about.

So how do you communicate innovative ideas and information in a business and cultural environment that shuns the complex?

What doesn't work

Faced with this dilemma, you might be tempted to swing to one of two extremes—to either over-explain intricate concepts or to reduce them to such basics that they lose most of their meaning. But as you may have experienced, either of those routes will lead straight to frustration, for both you and your audience.

Some daunting statistics about reader attention spans

- Average time spent on a web page: 15 seconds[1]
- Average time spent reading a marketing e-mail: 11.1 seconds[2]
- Average time spent reviewing a pitch deck: 3 minutes 44 seconds[3]

[1] 2014 study by the data analytics company Chartbeat. Tony Haile, "What You Think You Know About the Web is Wrong," (blog), TIME, March 9, 2014, https://time.com/12933/what-you-think-you-know-about-the-web-is-wrong/.

[2] 2017 study by Litmus Email Analytics. Chad White, "Email Attention Spans Increasing," (infographic), March 8, 2017, https://litmus.com/blog/email-attention-spans-increasing-infographic.

[3] Study conducted by DocSend and Harvard professor Tom Eisenmann. DocSend, What We Learned from 200 Startups Who Raised $360M, 2019, https://docsend.com/view/p8jxcr.

Figure 5.1 Page from a website giveaway with a simple visual design

Think also about the usability of your giveaway. For example, if you're creating a booklet of worksheets, the visual design should make them easy to fill out; you might want to provide a printable option for people who like writing in longhand and a fillable PDF for people who prefer to write with a keyboard. If you're offering a checklist, try to get all the items on a single page to simplify tracking. Or if you're creating a series of videos, provide transcripts for people who prefer reading to listening. The more user-friendly your giveaway, the better it shows how intently you care about your audience and the problem they face. And the more successfully you communicate your care and concern, the easier it is for your audience to believe in your wisdom, trust your advice, and become curious about your products and services.

Practical Tips from a Skilled Simplifier

Anirudh Koul is head of AI (artificial intelligence) & Research at Aira, a California-based startup that has created a seeing-eye app for the visually impaired. Aira enables people who are blind or nearly blind to interpret and navigate the world by using the phone's camera. The app interprets visual data from the camera's video feed and conveys it to the user through spoken language. For example, Aira can read a menu, describe people sitting in a boardroom, and give the layout of a grocery store.

As you can imagine, the sophisticated AI behind Aira defies simple explanation. And yet Anirudh prides himself on explaining deep machine learning for mobile devices to a range of audiences, from novices to those he calls "ninjas" (expert practitioners) and "gurus" (researchers). Over the past decade, Anirudh has gained extensive experience as a public speaker, at a range of conferences, including Tedx Seattle. This exposure to live audiences has taught him a lot about how to communicate complex concepts clearly and concisely.

Here are a few pointers from Anirudh's conference experience that apply particularly well to e-books and other resources you might create as website giveaways:

- **Simplify your key message.** Pare it down to "the essence of the message you want to pass through" and lose unnecessary details.
- **Write the way you speak.** "Most people," says Anirudh, "don't write the way they speak. They write the way they write." In other words, they write in a style that's more formal, and often more awkward, than their natural communication style. Take an easy shortcut to clarity by expressing yourself in a writing voice that echoes the vocabulary and rhythms of your natural speech.
- **Keep your sentences short and your word choices basic.** Whereas many communication experts advise writers to aim for a readability level of Grade 7 or 8, Anirudh goes further. He claims that his forthcoming book on AI is written in such a simple way that a fourth-grader could read it.

- **Work with your audience's agenda.** Anirudh's advice is to "Think of what the audience wants to listen to, not what you want to speak." As a conference speaker, his goal is to connect with his audience's interests so directly that they get excited and tell others about the ideas he's shared. And that's exactly what you want to happen when people read your website giveaway— you want your audience to find your resource so clear and compelling that they share the download link and recruit more subscribers to your e-mail list.
- **Communicate visually.** Anirudh's conference presentations integrate plenty of visuals, including infographics. This approach enables him to teach new concepts in ways that engage his audiences, without burdening them with overly technical terms. "People appreciate that they are learning, not that you are an expert," he explains.

   A true expert doesn't need to parade their knowledge; they demonstrate their expertise through their ability to make the complex accessible, and one of the best ways to do that is to make concepts and data visual.

Pointing to the Next Step

Creating a web giveaway requires an unselfish attitude, but it is hardly a selfless act. Your end goal, remember, is to turn web users into leads, leads into prospects whom you engage with regularly through your e-mail list, and prospects into customers.

To start that chain reaction, you need a strong closing call to action. Once you've enabled your audience to solve the particular problem your giveaway targets, it's time to let them know about other ways you can help. You might, for instance, direct them to a sales page for a related product or service or invite them to a free consultation call or your regular Facebook Live video series.

Offer your call to action in the same tone you use throughout your giveaway. It should, like the rest of that item, sound natural and genuinely friendly. Ideally, it moves your audience one step closer to two-way communication with you. Through visiting your website and viewing your giveaway, they've passively absorbed a lot of information from you. If those activities have generated enough curiosity and built enough trust, then some of your audience may be ready to interact with you live. So your call to action could, for example, invite them to phone your 1-800 number, attend a free webinar, or meet with you for a free consult.

Enjoy dreaming up and developing creative giveaways for your audience. For innovators and change-makers, there's no better marketing tool for sharing your mission and making a direct impact while you do it.

Examples of Creative Giveaways

Imagine you run a company that produces industrial-size batteries from sustainably sourced materials. Your customers and prospects are mainly manufacturers who must comply with new environmental regulations. They're concerned not just about the batteries used on their production lines but also about sustainability issues in general. Here are some examples of intriguing giveaways that could offer value to your audience:

- Seven Little-Known Secrets to Sustainable Manufacturing (PDF)
- How to Green Your Production Line: Your Step-by-Step Guide to Sustainability and Cost Savings (e-book)
- Three Inspiring Case Studies in Green Manufacturing (video series)
- Green Manufacturing Mini-course (online self-paced course)
- Checklist for Choosing a Sustainability Consultant (PDF)
- Whitepaper: How to Choose the Best Industrial Battery System for Your Plant (PDF)
- Manifesto for Green Manufacturers (PDF infographic)

I'd encourage you to start a folder of excellent giveaways you come across through your Internet surfing so you can emulate particular elements of them in your creations. I make a habit of downloading interesting freebies, even when the topic is not directly relevant to my audience, so I can scrutinize different aspects of them and copy what works well. You never know where you'll find inspiration for your next great headline, theme, visual design, or creative use of media.

Checklist for Website Giveaways

- ❑ Attention-grabbing headline
- ❑ Laser focus on a specific problem the target audience faces
- ❑ Practical information the audience can use to act on the specific problem
- ❑ Attractive visual design that complies with company branding
- ❑ Simple writing style that's easy to skim
- ❑ Conversational tone of a helpful guide
- ❑ Positive, can-do attitude that emphasizes the value of applying the information
- ❑ Strong call to action

CHAPTER 6

Blog Posts

Many entrepreneurs I meet through my consulting work feel the pressure of what I call "the blogging burden." They know that blogging would help increase their visibility, showcase their expertise, and cultivate relationships with their target audience. But committing to regularly publishing content just seems so arduous. Where do you find good ideas? How do you craft content that will resonate with your audience? And, of course, where on earth do you find the writing time?

In this chapter, we'll knock down some common barriers that prevent entrepreneurs from establishing a strong online platform for their business. You'll learn how to define your blog and your blog voice, how to generate topics, and how to create a strategic blogging calendar. You'll soon discover that blogging offers you one of the most flexible and fun ways to connect with your audience, and working blog-writing into your weekly schedule is easier than you might think.

Your Blog, Your Way

The word "blog" is a rather shapeless word that makes me think of "blob." I know it's short for "web log," but what the heck is that? Unlike more established kinds of writing, such as reports or proposals, the blog lacks any kind of standard definition. There are no hard-edged requirements to guide you as you generate posts and weave them into a cohesive online publication.

That lack of established guidance can create a sense of overwhelm—unless you look at its flip side. Because there's no Worldwide Blogging Authority to tell you what your blog could or should look like, you're free to give it the form that best suits you and your audience. Once you define what blogging means for you, you're able to give yourself your own guidelines, and that structure simplifies the process of choosing topics, generating ideas, and producing content.

To define blogging your way, use the PAVE method. Spend some time exploring these four questions:

- **What is your PURPOSE for the blog?** What do you want your blog to achieve? Frame your answer as specific outcome statements that begin with verbs.

- **Who is your ideal AUDIENCE?** If you've created avatars for your website, then you may able to use them to define your blog audience. (If you haven't yet created your avatars, check out Chapter 4.) Or you may want your blog to target an audience that's narrower than your website audience.

- **What VALUE do you want to offer?** Your blog provides a great way for you to demonstrate your expertise, but your audience will take the time to read it only if it delivers *immediate value*. Immediate value means information and insights they can apply right away, without buying your product or service.

- **How do you want to ENGAGE with your audience?** Your blog could offer superbly helpful content tailored to the precise needs and interests of your audience, but if it doesn't foster *direct engagement*, then it won't repay your effort. Consider the different ways you could integrate calls to action into your blog posts. For example, you could invite your audience to:
  - Connect with you via social media
  - Download a web giveaway on a related topic
  - Book a free consult
  - Respond to a poll
  - Share a comment
  - Submit a question to be addressed in another post

Once you've answered the four PAVE questions, you should be able to draft a brief mission statement for your blog.

For example:

> The PURPOSE of my blog is to build an online community of people committed to replacing physical gifts with gift-experiences. My AUDIENCE comprises people of various age groups (primarily 20- and 30-somethings) who are committed to a zero-waste lifestyle, earn more than $60,000 a year, and live in urban centers across the United States. I offer the VALUE of practical ways to rethink the various ways we celebrate special occasions. I plan to ENGAGE with my audience by inviting them to download free resources, share Instagram posts of creative gift-experiences they have given or received, and participate in polls.

Such a statement provides the structure and writing guidelines to "pave" the way for you to generate on-brand, on-target posts that will wow your audience and woo them to you.

Defining Your Blog Voice

When we think about "brand identity," our mind tends to go straight to graphic design. But writing style also plays an important role in shaping the impression people form of your organization. Defining the kind of blog you'll create gives you a great opportunity to dive into the design of your brand voice, your company's writing personality.

Your brand voice comes across through the many different style choices you make as you produce written content. If you've read the chapter on website giveaways (Chapter 5), then you've already started to contemplate some of those choices. You've thought about the kind of "helper profile" you'd like to create when you're offering free advice and about the particular communication style such a helper should use. Now it's time to take that thinking deeper by designing the voice for your overall brand.

We'll borrow a technique from graphic designers, the brand board. When graphic designers construct a brand identity, they collect various visual elements that resonate with the brand owner and assemble them on a digital or paper board. That way, the brand owner can see at a glance the key elements that define their organization visually such as the logo, primary and secondary fonts, primary and secondary color palettes, icons, and so on.

You can take a similar approach to describing your brand's voice identity. Follow these steps to create a writing brand board:

1. **Identify three to five key words that describe the personality of your company.** Write those in the center of your page or screen and circle each word.

2. **Brainstorm words that you associate with the way a person with that personality speaks.** Cluster these voice descriptors around your five key words.

3. **Add images of people who speak and/or write in a way that embodies your voice descriptors.** You can draw the images or use photos. Your images can be real people, dead or alive, or fictional characters. If your imagination leads you to celebrities, talking animals, or a 15th-century inventor, then by all means include them.

4. **Include voice clips of brands you admire.** Add sentences or short paragraphs from websites and blogs you admire because their writing personality aligns with the voice you'd like to create.

Once you've created your writing brand board, take some time to reflect on it. If you're a solopreneur, you may want to journal about the experience of creating the board, your interpretation of the final product, and the practical guidelines it provides. If your team has helped create the brand board, be sure to debrief on the insights it has delivered and to capture those learnings as best practices for anyone blogging or producing writing on behalf of the company.

Now that you've defined your brand, it will take practice to implement it consistently. One of the best ways to develop your writing style is to emulate the style of others. For centuries, this was the way most educators taught writing, and even today creative writing instructors often use this approach. For instance, budding novelists might be asked to write a passage as if they were Ernest Hemingway or Toni Morrison. You can apply this tried-and-true learning method by using your voice clips, or other samples from the brands they represent, as models as you craft blog posts.

How to Generate Hot Blog Topics

When I meet someone who's experiencing "blogging burden," they're often worried about delivering regular content to their audience because they can't imagine coming up with fresh, valuable content at least once a week. Two fintech entrepreneurs from Halifax, Canada, have found a way to overcome that hurdle, using a data-driven approach. Their key advice: "It's all about the process."

Karen Lightstone and Laurie Sinclair are two long-time friends with a shared passion for helping entrepreneurs make their businesses more profitable. Karen teaches accounting in the Sobey School of Business at Saint Mary's University. Laurie has a consulting background and now works for a not-for-profit organization that empowers women entrepreneurs. Together, Karen and Laurie created Finazz (www.finazz.com), a cloud-based application that makes it easy for entrepreneurs to view and interpret their financial data.

The Finazz founders approach blogging with a systematic approach you'd expect from an accountant and a consultant. Rather than leaving it up to the blogging muse to inspire their posts, they collect and analyze market data to guide their planning.

Working with a digital marketing strategist, Laurie and Karen have researched key words a customer might use when looking for solutions to some of the problems Finazz addresses, such as not understanding why take-home income is low even when sales are up. These key words serve as launching points for brainstorming specific blog posts. For instance, because so many entrepreneurs have trouble understanding "revenue" and "profits," an upcoming post will bear the headline "Revenue is for vanity; profit is for sanity."

Karen and Laurie also use conversations with entrepreneurs in their community as input. For instance, Karen experienced an aha moment when a business owner proudly showed her a new revenue-tracking app, which he believed gave him all the financial information he needed to know, although it gave him insight only into how much money he was taking in, not how much he was spending. Through her work with women entrepreneurs, Laurie also gets daily insight into both the pain points business owners experience related to financial data and the hidden issues they're unaware of.

As Finazz posts blog articles, Karen and Laurie use web analytics tools to track the audience's response, and then they use that data to develop future posts. Focusing on what the data tells them about their readers enables them to view their blog content from the customer vantage point, something that's tough to do. Laurie explains: "When you are innovative and create something, it takes a long time, and you're so in it that things are so very obvious to you. It's very hard to change your thinking to understand how someone else is viewing it."

Planning Your Blogging Time

Halfway through my interview with Finazz, as the cofounders recall stories about entrepreneurs who are out of touch with their "numbers," Karen grabs a notepad and starts recording new ideas for blog themes and headlines. Later, working with their digital marketing strategist, Laurie and she will add those ideas to their calendar of upcoming blog posts, which forms part of their overall social media plan.

The Finazz blogging calendar gives Karen and Laurie a strategic tool to guide their content development. Because it's based on audience data, it provides ready-made topics business owners should find pertinent and engaging. Rather than waiting for creative inspiration to strike, Karen and Laurie simply look to the calendar for direction.

This strategic, market-centered approach not only helps prevent writer's block. It also overcomes one of the most common mistakes Laurie sees entrepreneurs commit, thinking that "they are the driver of their business." But, says Laurie, "It's not about you." Customers drive your revenue, so smart business owners look to them to drive all other aspects of the business too. Creating a data-driven blogging calendar ensures that your customers, not your personal whims, are driving your blog.

To set up your own calendar, you may want to configure an Excel spreadsheet like the example on the next page. If you prefer to work by hand, you can also use a paper calendar or even a piece of loose-leaf. Or you might want to check out some of the free templates offered by social media consultants and providers of social media tools. (Hubspot offers a particularly rich resource library.)

Start by producing a list of key words and phrases related to problems your customers recognize and want to solve. Use these to generate a list of monthly themes for the next two to three months. Organizing a month's worth of content around a set theme helps create continuity and cohesiveness so that your blog functions as a unified online publication, not just a collection of random articles. Monthly themes also make it easy for you to link blog posts to sales events, such as product launches and seasonal promotions.

With your monthly themes in place, you can then generate post topics and, if you're really on a roll, some of your headlines. If you're integrating your blogging calendar with a comprehensive social media plan, then look for opportunities to align blog content with other social media postings.

Figure 6.1 shows part of a strategic blogging calendar developed in an Excel spreadsheet.

Blogging Calendar, Q1 2020

Monthly theme	Post date	Topic	Headline	Audience response
JAN				
Internet of Things applications in healthcare	2	Diabetes management	Three new smart devices that will reduce the number of diabetes checkups by 40%	122 views, 3 comments
	9	Heart monitoring	Move over Pandora: Next-gen wearable heart monitors look like fine jewellery	
	16	Ingestible sensors, connected inhalers, bluetooth blood pressure cuffs	Why "non-compliance" is about to go the way of the dodo bird	

Figure 6.1 Strategic blogging calendar

Once you start using your calendar to generate full blog posts, scheduling your writing sessions becomes automatic. Your customers drive your content, and your pre-booked content drives your regular writing sessions. With a system in place, you no longer have to rely on random bursts of the creative impulse to produce high-quality posts.

Your calendar also functions as a tracking tool. Use it to record your final headlines and document the audience response. The more closely you keep your eye on how your audience interacts with your blog, the easier you'll find it to produce engaging content on a regular schedule. No need to worry about running out of ideas. Just keep tuning into your customers' problems and paying attention to the language they use to talk about them, and you'll never lack for engaging blog content.

Seven Key Practices for Creating Compelling Posts

So far, you've defined the kind of blog you're producing, described your brand voice, and established a system for generating two to three months' worth of topics at time. Now, let's get down to the nitty-gritty of crafting blog posts. Here are seven key practices that will help you turn a topic for a post into a fully developed article that grabs your audience's attention and encourages them to engage with you beyond the blog.

1. **Obsess over your headline.** As you'll recall from Chapter 3, most effective headlines actually follow a proven formula, so take time to study the formulas and learn how to apply them to your situation. Also think about how your headline can evoke a specific emotion. Curiosity, fear, surprise, and desire prove particularly powerful levers to pull.

2. **Create visual appeal.** An arresting visual creates an emotional "hook" to lure your reader into the body of your post. A relevant, emotionally resonant visual can also suggest metaphors or concepts to explore in your post. No budget for images? Check out Pixabay and Unsplash, two of my favorite online sources of free high-resolution photos.

3. **Show proof of value up front.** Blog writing is the art of continual seduction. First, you lure your audience with a strong headline. Then you intrigue them with an appealing image. Next, in your first paragraph, you show them the value the post as a whole will deliver.

   Some bloggers fall into the trap of thinking that holding their main idea back for the end of a post will build suspense and keep the audience's attention. But a blog post is not a detective novel. Remember the impatient insect brain of our typical web user? "Sticky" blog posts state the main idea up front to convince users that the rest of the post merits their sustained attention.

4. **Vary the format of your posts.** Keep that buzzing insect brain busy by keeping it guessing as to the kind of article you'll post. Here are a few different article types to consider as you plan your calendar:
   - How-to article
   - Op-ed piece on an issue affecting your field, industry, or community
   - Listicle (article in the form of a list)
   - Book review
   - Article by a guest blogger
   - Challenge of a popular assumption or myth

- Case study
- Insider secrets

5. **Include examples and stories.** Regardless of the overall article format, spice up your content by incorporating examples and stories your audience will find relatable and persuasive. Become a story hunter, someone always on the lookout for great stories. Like Karen and Laurie, you might find stories through interactions with your target market. You might also tap into your life experience or draw on myths and folk tales.

6. **Chunk and label.** Make it easy for users to skim and scroll through your content. "Chunk" your content into short paragraphs, lists, and charts and visuals (if appropriate). Label each chunk by providing a heading or subheading. Your users, especially those viewing your blog from a mobile device, will appreciate being able to preview your content at a glance and absorb it quickly.

7. **Emulate models.** To become an all-star blogger, seek out popular blogs in your field or a related domain, analyze their content, and intentionally copy the approach. Here are some questions to help you identify aspects of your model blogs you can copy in your own posts:
    - How long is the average post? (This can vary widely, and there's no best practice that fits all situations. Keep in mind, though, that Google will only pick up on your content if your post runs to at least 300 words.)
    - What kinds of articles does the blog include most often?
    - What other kinds of articles does it feature?
    - What headline formulas do posts use?
    - How would you describe the voice of the blog?
    - What style choices do you notice?
    - How is graphic design applied to the blog (e.g., layout, font variations, color, visuals)?
    - How do posts encourage the audience to engage with the company?

Here's an example of a short blog post you can use to start your collection of articles to examine and emulate (Figure 6.2).

Four Completely Self-gratifying Reasons to Test-drive an Electric Vehicle

Making a green purchase always brings a certain kind of moral pleasure. It feels good to do the right thing by the environment, even if that means paying more for a slightly less satisfactory product.

At least that's been the story environmentally conscious car buyers have had to tell themselves until now. But with the unveiling of next year's fleet of electric vehicles (EVs), that's about to change. The 2020 line-up of EVs, both domestic and foreign, features cars that deliver stellar performance and a driving experience you can't get from a gasoline-powered vehicle unless you're training for the Indy 500.

So forget about the delayed gratification of knowing that buying a green vehicle makes a small contribution to the fight against climate change. Instead, embrace these three entirely self-indulgent reasons for switching your drive to an EV:

1. **Smooth ride.** We tested three EVs on the back roads of Northern Oregon: the Nissan Leaf, the Chevrolet Bolt, and the Jaguar I-PACE. We expected the Jaguar to deliver a jolt-free ride, and it didn't disappoint; we might have been sailing or floating rather than driving. But what we didn't expect was the silky smooth performance of the Bolt and Leaf, both of which easily outperform conventional vehicles in their price range ($37 to $42,000).
2. **Silent engine.** Enjoy your vehicle's stereo, unmuffled by the cacophony of a piston-driven gasoline engine. Hold a conversation with your child in the back seat without having to yell over your shoulder. Even at speeds above 60 mph, EVs glide along the highway in quiet serenity.
3. **Awesome acceleration.** Can you say "instant torque"? Yes, instant. Even the cheapest car we test-drove, the Bolt, took us from 0 to 60 in just under six seconds. The BMW i-8 got us there in 4.5 seconds. Owning an EV could be the closest the ordinary citizen comes to living the NASCAR dream.
4. **Luxury-class comfort.** Even the humble Bolt boasts an interior you'd normally find in a car with a much higher price tag. Most EVs come with standard leather seats, high-end stereo systems, Apple CarPlay or Android Auto, and passenger video screens. These cars are built for drivers, but passengers will savor the ride too.

Curious to take an EV for a spin? Sign up for our next test-drive event, at the Barney Ridge Arena on Nov 15th.

This photo taken from a "first-person perspective", enables the reader to picture themselves in the driver's seat, enjoying the fantastic driving experience electric vehicles offer.

This headline follows a classic formula: *X reasons*.... It also rouses curiosity by including an adjective not usually associated with green buying decisions: "self-gratifying."

The post's main idea appears near the beginning of the article.

The voice of the post is consistently direct and authoritative yet light-hearted. The slightly playful style helps engage readers.

Bold running heads make the article easy to skim.

Notice the short sentences, here and throughout the post. Short, simple sentences sound conversational and are easy to skim.

This short post clocks in at just 389 words, just over the minimum Google requires to register a post in its databases. There's no "rule" about how long a blog post should be. You may want to vary the length of your articles and monitor the audience response. Plus, variety in a blog is a good way to keep readers interested.

The first-person pronoun "We" humanizes the company voice of the blog.

Casual language and informal punctuation creates a voice that sounds energetic and relatable.

The call to action provides a way for readers to engage with the company.

Figure 6.2 Sample blog post

Great blogs don't just happen through creative serendipity; they develop through audience-focused intention and repeated practice. Follow the seven recommendations above, along with the other strategies and tips you've learned in this chapter, and you'll be well on your way to establishing the powerful online presence your company deserves.

Checklist for Blog Posts

❑ Content aligned with the way the blog has been defined in terms of the PAVE method:
  ○ What is the PURPOSE for the blog?
  ○ Who is the ideal AUDIENCE?
  ○ What VALUE do you want to offer?
  ○ How do you want to ENGAGE with your audience?
❑ Distinct, consistent blog voice, aligned with the brand identity
❑ Topic related to key words that resonate with the target audience
❑ Topic relevant to the monthly theme (if applicable)
❑ Attention-grabbing headline
❑ Emotionally resonant visual(s)
❑ Strong first paragraph that states the post's main idea
❑ Post format that creates variety in the blog
❑ Vivid example or story to bring the ideas to life
❑ Content chunked and labeled for easy skimming
❑ Call to action encouraging audience engagement

CHAPTER 7

Grant Applications and Proposals

My education in the art of writing grant applications and proposals began with not just one failure but two. As a PhD student at the University of Toronto, I applied twice for a coveted scholarship from the Social Sciences and Research Council of Canada (now worth $35,000 a year) and was disappointed to find my submission was rejected both times.

"Disappointment" is actually an understatement. When I got the rejection notices in the mail, I felt shocked, dismayed, wounded to the core. My pride was seriously injured because, with a string of academic awards behind me, I thought I'd mastered the art of the scholarship applications. I'd carefully read and re-read the application booklet, drafted and redrafted my essays, and proofed the final copy multiple times. Baffled and hurt, I kept asking myself, "What did I do wrong?"

In hindsight, I see that what I did wrong was to focus on the application form rather than on the people reading it. At that stage in my academic career, I did not yet understand that scholarship happens as a conversation among scholars. So I gave little thought to the professors on the evaluation committee and focused on what you might call the technical content of my grant proposal, such as the books I planned to read and the ideas I planned to explore.

By the time I'd reached the third year of my PhD program, I'd become more familiar with the way scholarship works. I recognized that I needed to show the evaluation committee the unique contribution my research would make to the field. Rather than discussing my ideas as if they existed in a vacuum, I showed how they would build on the work of others and address glaring gaps in the existing body of knowledge. In other words, I made a strong case for the value of my proposed research.

I also explained my research plan in terms nonexperts could understand since I knew the committee would comprise professors not just from my discipline (English) but also from other fields in the humanities. My descriptions of the methods I intended to use and the results I hoped to produce had to be intelligible to an economist or a philosopher or a political scientist with no understanding of literary theory.

Since this would be my last shot at the prize, I also threw aside the cautious, tentative tone I'd used in my previous applications. Instead, I wrote as if I'd already received the funding and mapped out my plan in bold language. "Would" and "could" became "will" as I envisioned my research unfolding phase by phase, displacing old models and creating fresh knowledge.

My new approach worked. And I came away from the application process not just with funding for the final two years of my PhD studies but also with valuable lessons in what it really takes to sell a group of people on your vision. I learned how to zero in on a significant problem, write for multiple stakeholders, avoid "tell-all syndrome," and paint a compelling vision of success. These are the lessons we'll dive into in this chapter.

A Note about Terminology

While this chapter addresses both grants and proposals, I'll use "proposals" as shorthand for both types of documents. That works because grant applications really form a subset of proposals that fulfill these criteria:

- Target an established program run by a government, charitable, or not-for-profit organization.
- Aim to raise nonrepayable funds.
- Meet specific qualification requirements pertaining to both the applicant and the proposed work.
- Follow a set structure, often presented as a form with set word counts per section.
- Include reporting requirements.

Because program guidelines dictate the structure and format for a grant application, grant applications may look different from proposals. But the purpose is the same: to secure permission and resources to complete a specific project.

Grant applications fall into the broader category of solicited, formal proposals. A proposal created in response to a Request For Proposals is also both solicited (the organization has asked for submissions) and formal (there's a set structure to follow and specific criteria to fulfill).

As an entrepreneur, you'll no doubt draft your share of such templated documents. But you'll probably spend more of your proposal-writing time on solicited, informal proposals. These documents typically evolve as you guide a prospect through your sales process. After one or more preliminary conversations to assess the prospect's needs, you'll describe in writing how you can help fill those needs and what such help will cost.

Informal proposals are shape-shifters whose contours are determined by the context, the size of the project, and the target audience. They can take the form of a short e-mail, a slide presentation, a one-pager, a video, or a document running to 10 or more pages. Beneath this seeming amorphousness, however, most winning proposals conform to a basic structure; they present a painful, urgent problem and describe a specific solution to resolve it.

Start by Pinpointing Your Problem

"Problem" seems like such a negative word that we often go to great lengths to avoid it. To avoid blaming, we tend to talk about "issues," "concerns," and "glitches" rather than using the P-word. In fact, when I'm coaching people on how to write effective e-mails, I warn them against using "problem" because, especially in online communication, it can set off instant alarm bells.

But persuasive grant applications and proposals must start by sounding the alarm. Otherwise, there's no reason for your readers to consider an alternative to their *status quo*. Keep in mind that we humans are highly adaptable, and we can adapt to the most miserable of conditions. That means that even though you might consider your prospect's circumstances as unbearably problematic, your readers may have grown so comfortable with their discomfort as to barely feel it. Your task is to identify their precise pain and enable them to feel how much it's really hurting them.

That doesn't mean using overly emotional language or exaggerating the size and impact of a threat. A thorough, realistic appraisal of the problem's scope and urgency will gain respect and trust, whereas an over-blown depiction of nightmare scenarios will get you the reputation of a fear-mongerer or worse.

While I'm not a big fan of talk-show psychology, I think one of Dr. Phil's routine moves makes a great model for proposal writers. As you may have seen, Dr. Phil often begins a session with a client by asking them to describe their current situation and how they're dealing with it. Then—with just the right dramatic timing—he quips, "How's that working for you?"

Dr. Phil could start off by telling the client outright what's not working for them. But by first listening to the client explain their situation in their own words, he gains their trust. He also disarms their defenses. His question doesn't blame or shame. It simply asks the client to pause and reflect, to see their problem and their coping strategies through fresh eyes so they can truly recognize the mess they're caught up in.

In the first part of your proposal, you're trying to achieve a similar effect. First, you want to gain your prospect's trust by showing them how well you've listened to the challenges they've shared with you. Depending on the situation, that sharing may have happened through the program description for a grant, through an RFP, or through conversations with the potential client or customer. You show how carefully you've paid attention by echoing back to the prospect the language they've used to describe their distress.

For example, let's say you're applying for a grant to restore a heritage cottage using a new environmentally friendly paint your company produces. You notice that the program description on the Heritage Society's web page encourages applications from "organizations that share the Society's values of sustainable, cost-effective restoration practices." Although most of your marketing collateral describes your product line as "green," "clean," or "pro-environment," you take the cue and refer to "sustainable paint products" throughout your application.

Once you've gained your prospect's trust by showing how deeply you understand their situation, you can then make the Dr. Phil move. You can do this by summarizing some of the ways the prospect has tried to solve their problem. For instance, maybe the Heritage Society has previously tried to restore building interiors by using chalk-based paint, but it soon faded. Or perhaps they've considered the leading environmentally friendly paint on the consumer market, but it's much pricier than your commercial-grade product. To set the stage for your solution, you'll want to remind the prospect that none of the solutions they've tried have met their values of sustainability and cost-effectiveness. Clearly, it's time for a new approach.

What Do You Do When Your Audience Doesn't Recognize the Problem?

When you're selling an innovative product or service, the existing problem may not be readily apparent. Sometimes the need doesn't really show itself until the solution becomes obvious.

For instance, picture yourself living on the outskirts of Dayton, Ohio, back in 1903, five years before America's first affordable automobile, Ford's Model T, rolled off the assembly line. At this point, you're used to traveling short distances by horse and buggy. Once or twice a year, you take the railroad to visit family who live several states away, but for most trips to and from Dayton, your old mare and four-wheeled carriage work just fine, thanks. You can't imagine ever needing any other mode of transportation.

If I tried to sell you on an automobile by describing how fast and far it could go, you'd brush me aside quicker than your mare swishes horse-flies away with her tail. You don't recognize that you have either a speed problem or a distance problem, so pitching you a speed-and-distance solution will waste my time as well as yours. Before I can convince you that I have the best solution, I first need to reveal your problem.

In many cases, an unrevealed problem shows up as a missed opportunity. For example, let's say your wife sells herbs and herb jellies at the market in downtown Dayton on Saturday mornings. She'd like to make more jars of jelly each week, but her production time is limited because it takes her an hour to travel from your home to the market (and an hour back again). Her cousin in a nearby town has also encouraged her to sell her goods in their market, but it's too far away (more than 90 minutes one way). Once you and I start discussing your wife's businesses and the opportunities she's losing out on, suddenly you have both a speed and a distance problem. Now, you're primed to learn about the amazing solution I have to offer: the horseless carriage.

Writing for Multiple Stakeholders

"Framing" is the key word to keep in mind as you develop proposals. When a solution has been designed to fit a specific market need, it's easy to fall into the trap of believing it will "sell itself." But context matters. The way you frame the problem for your particular audience will make the difference between proposal success and failure.

Cognitive linguist George Lakoff describes frames as "mental structures that shape the way we see the world."[1] Those structures exist in our brains as neural connections forged through our experience, but we are mostly unaware of them. They operate at the subconscious level, and they are extremely influential, predetermining our response to new stimuli, including new ideas and information.

To enable your audience to view your proposed solution from your perspective, you must work within, and sometimes shift, their mental framing. Only once you recognize the frame an audience brings to a situation can you position your ideas so they fit within that frame. Or alternatively, you might need to articulate a new frame to help your audience interpret your ideas the way you want them to be interpreted.

When you're writing for multiple stakeholders, as is almost always the case with a grant application or proposal, you're likely dealing with multiple frames. The key is to create a frame that will appeal to all of them and enable them to embrace a common vision.

It takes political savvy to do that, and a lot of off-the-page effort, which involves both detective work and relationship-building.

1. Do Your Detective Work

The kind of detective work I'm talking about involves sleuthing out power relationships among your audience. In the case of a grant application or RFP, try to find out all you can about the committee members' vetting applications. It's fair game to call up a charitable or government organization and ask who's on the committee this year. If they're reluctant to share that information, you can ask about the typical composition of the

---

[1] G. Lakoff. *The All New Don't Think of an Elephant!* (White River Junction, VT: Chelsea Green Publishing, 2014), Introduction, Kindle.

committee. For instance, the Heritage Society committee might typically comprise one or two donors, a member of City Council, the executive director of the Society (or her delegate), a contractor, and a volunteer who helps out in the Society archives.

For RFPs, the detective work can be more challenging. Read the RFP carefully so you respect the guidelines it sets out. Some RFPs encourage people to call with questions, while others forbid it. Regardless of the RFP "rules," you can leverage your professional network. Use the grapevine to make some subtle inquiries about the organization's expectations and the typical make-up of the review panel.

If you're writing an informal proposal, however, you're in luck, Sherlock. Conversations with the client should give you ample opportunity to explore questions such as these:

- Who will decide whether the proposal is a go or no-go? (This is your Decision-maker.)
- Who else will read the proposal? (These are your Secondary Readers.)
- Who else could influence the decision? (These are your Influencers, and you may find them outside and inside the organization.)
- For each stakeholder group, what outcome from the proposal will matter most to them? What will matter least to them?
- What key words will resonate with each stakeholder group?

When you're creating an informal proposal for a client you've met, some of your detective work can take a direct approach. When I'm proposing writing training to a CEO, for example, I normally ask outright who else in the organization will be reading the proposal. I also ask whether there's any specific information they'd like to see in the proposal. Most clients appreciate this question because they know it will enable me to tailor the proposal to the interests of their team, making it easier for them to review the document and make a decision.

Other aspects of proposal detective work tend to require a more indirect approach. For instance, it's not always wise to ask Secondary Readers and Influencers what their number-one goal for the project is because some of their interests may conflict with those of other readers. Such proposal intelligence is best teased out through listening attentively, researching your audience online, and observing body language and personal interactions during meetings.

2. Build Relationships Off-page

Kevin Canning has a PhD in physiology and is currently VP of Science Strategy, Portfolio and Operations for The Green Organic Dutchman, a cannabis producer with head offices in Toronto, Canada. With more than 15 years of industry experience under his belt, Kevin has learned the hard way that writing for audiences of multiple stakeholders can take a writer deep into "a political chess game." It's crucial, he says, to figure out the personalities of the different players and to learn who your "allies" are. In Kevin's experience, which spans a variety of industries, "selling" a project idea begins long before any writing happens.

At one stage in his career, Kevin watched an important recommendation report (a close cousin to the proposal) flop because the author failed to pre-sell his ideas. At the time, Kevin was working for a Chinese organization, where the usual "political chess game" we find in North American organizations was complicated by a rigid hierarchy and a significant lack of transparency. To communicate effectively in that environment, Kevin found himself needing to adapt a whole new set of practices. Before writing an important document, he would first hold a live conversation. After the discussion, the document he created would simply confirm what had already been decided.

This cross-cultural survival strategy actually works well in most proposal situations. Try to make your customer or client your partner in creating the proposal. Ask about the kind of information that will help them make a decision and find out their preferred way to see that presented. You'll be surprised at how forthcoming most clients will be. I've had clients tell me straight up, "Give me a table with three options at such-and-such price points" or "Make sure there's enough background to allow the COO to understand the rationale for the project." Then all I need to do is deliver on what we've outlined together.

Kevin recalls a dramatic example of a persuasive document that misfired because the writer didn't invest time in this kind of relationship-building with the client. The situation took place in China, and the proposal writer was an English physician who wrote a report recommending that four divisions of the company merge. The recommendations were well-researched and clearly presented, but because the physician hadn't taken the time to get to know the stakeholders personally, his ideas were dismissed out of hand. To make matters worse, the leaders of the different stakeholder groups reacted so negatively to the report that they formed organizational silos to protect their individual domains.

Taking the time to build relationships with your proposal readers will not only prevent such instant rejection. It will also enable you to avoid a hazard that undermines many technical proposals: a tendency to over-elaborate and provide irrelevant information that distracts from your main points.

Avoid "Tell-all Syndrome"

Because it takes so much effort to develop a proposal, it's tempting to create a one-size-fits-all document that will suit various situations. Writers who take that route tend to hedge their bets by including in their boilerplate all the features and benefits that could possibly appeal to someone interested in their product or service. But this comprehensive approach rarely yields results because the particular stakeholders reading the document are looking for particular information relevant to their needs. They're not willing to waste time sifting through details that don't matter to them.

Proposals must, above all, be personal. Clients are looking for proof that you've listened to their needs and have taken the time to tailor your usual "spiel" to their situation. Bear in mind that each client believes their situation to be truly unique. Yes, you may have seen similar circumstances a dozen times, but if you want your readers to pay attention to what you have to say, you must acknowledge their specialness. That means carefully selecting the information you share with them so they can easily see how well what you're proposing maps to their specific needs and goals.

Avoid "tell-all syndrome" by concentrating on the following questions as you draft your proposal:

- What are the top three to five benefits most relevant to the stakeholders' strategic goals?

- Which features attach to those specific benefits?
- Which benefits are least relevant (or completely irrelevant) to the stakeholders?
- Which features would the stakeholders probably use only rarely, if at all?

Your goal should be to thoughtfully curate the list of features and benefits you present so that you're showcasing those aspects of your proposed solution that will appeal most strongly to your target audience. Let your audience know this is your approach; they'll appreciate your consideration. If you're worried about omitting information that could influence the decision process, you can always include nonessential details in an appendix.

Another key strategy for making sure you don't overwhelm your readers with unnecessary detail is to create multiple stakeholder pathways through your document. Insert headings and subheadings so readers with different interests can hop and skip through the document following their own agenda. Also use overview statements at the beginning of each document section so readers can easily skim over sections they don't care about. For a document longer than five pages, be sure to include a table of contents and executive summary, two more aids to quick-and-easy navigation.

Create a Compelling Vision of Success

A proposal takes your audience on a journey from their present state, where they're living with the burden of a serious problem, to a future state, where the burden has been lifted, thanks to your help. The more vivid you can make this contrast between the current and future states, the better.

Paint a word-picture of the future state that enables readers to visualize what success will look like. Here are five different ways to do that:

1. **Lead with results.** Don't wait until the end of the proposal to reveal what the future will look like. Give a preview of that blissful state early in the document so you can refer to it as a recurring theme.

2. **Use concrete language.** Wherever possible, quantify your claims about the future. Rather than mentioning a "significant" increase in profit, for example, say that most clients you've worked with have increased their profits by at least 10 percent.

3. **Align specific parts of the solution with specific parts of the problem.** This tip assumes you've painted a detailed description of the problem. Once you've done that, you can map each component of the problem directly to the proposed solution. For instance, let's say the problems you're targeting pertain to the fabric currently being used in hip braces. Your problem description highlights two particularly frustrating elements of the problem: current fabrics start to deteriorate after only a few weeks, and they hold body odor. Your solution description should, therefore, speak directly to these two points. It should emphasize the durability of your fabric and its hygienic, odor-free qualities.

4. **Focus on impact.** This is especially critical if what you're proposing is something intangible, such as a software application or a service. Include examples and user-oriented descriptions to make your proposal concrete. For example, imagine you're writing a proposal for a music-streaming service similar to Spotify. Even though your service can't be seen or touched, you can describe the observable, measurable results it delivers—it allows users to stream music at so many bits per second.

5. **Clearly state what to expect.** Explain exactly how the proposed project will unfold or how the proposed product will be delivered and installed. Provide all the information your stakeholders will need to make their decision, such as:
   - Approach or methodology
   - Timeline
   - Deliverables
   - Team members
   - Costs
   - Other resources required
   - Risks and risk mitigation (if appropriate)
   - Answers to anticipated objections

To Produce Persuasive Proposals,
Tap into Your Creativity

When you're typing information into the boxes of a grant application form or spelling out exactly how you'll meet the requirements of an RFP, proposal writing can feel constrained. But don't let formatting and technical specifications bog you down because one of the keys to creating a powerful proposal is to tap into your creative side. Drawing on your creativity enables you to empathize with your audience, develop attention-grabbing visuals, and produce a compelling vision of what they can achieve through buying your product or service.

Dave Belt is a musician and serial entrepreneur whose ventures have included a record label, an alpaca farm in the Rocky Mountains, a restaurant, and his current business, a lavender farm on the North shore of Nova Scotia, Canada. Dave's varied experiences across different industries and regions have taught him that proposal writing is "a unique skill unto itself." Here's his top piece of advice: "The number one thing is you have to have the skill and creative ability to think from the perspective of the recipient of your information."

Before delivering a presentation or tackling a piece of writing, Dave spends time stepping into his audience's shoes—or moccasins, as the case may be. He recalls a delicate situation in which he was asked to talk to a Mi'kmaq band council about agritourism. He didn't want to walk on to the stage as "the white guy coming up to lecture," so he learned how to greet the crowd in Mi'kmaq and started his talk with a formal acknowledgment that he was speaking on unceded Mi'kmaq territory. With these trust-building moves, "I had their rapt attention," says Dave.

Practicing such creative empathy can help you craft proposals that speak to your audience in terms that resonate with their interests and needs. Your creativity can also help you grab your audience's attention through eye-catching visuals. Page after page of black-and-white text won't capture your readers' attention, warns Dave. Where formatting requirements allow, a strong proposal creates visual appeal by including headers, colored elements, charts, diagrams, and perhaps even stock photos to liven up the reading experience.

Finally, unleashing your creativity will allow you to articulate the successful future your proposal will usher in for your audience. When he's composing a piece of music, Dave describes his process as "creating an imaginary world." That's the same way I'd describe the job of a proposal writer: you must enable your audience to step into a vision of the future you can help them create. The more specific examples you can provide, the more real that vision will seem, and the more inspired your readers will be to pursue it with you.

Close on a Collaborative Note

Congratulations! You've written a persuasive proposal, and your stakeholders have read all the way to the end. Thanks to your carefully tailored content, they like what they've read, and they're ready to act—if you give them a slight nudge.

Just as a web page or a marketing e-mail closes with a call to action, a winning proposal provides a strong conclusion. Depending on the context and level of formality, you can do this through one or more of these closing techniques:

- Summarize your problem-to-solution message.
- Reiterate the positive impact the solution will produce.
- List your contact information.
- Sketch the two to three next steps that would be required to activate the proposal.
- Suggest possible times for a follow-up conversation.

In most business situations, a proposal serves a stepping-stone leading from a sales conversation to a contract negotiation. My favorite way to close an informal proposal, then, is to ask for a conversation to discuss the suggested ideas. If you're responding to an RFP, you won't have this luxury as your submission will follow a certain protocol. But if you have the opportunity to engage the client in further conversation, make the most of it. The more collaborative you appear, the more trust you'll foster. Position yourself as a partner in the proposal process, rather than a bidder, and the client will begin to view you as one of the team long before you get to the contracting stage. Figure 7.1 shows an example of a grant application that follows this approach.

Roseway Cottage Needs Repainting

The Roseway Cottage at 145 Brule Street stands as an important reminder of the lasting legacy of the Arts and Crafts movement in late-19th-century New England. As the only pre-20th-century residential building west of downtown, it draws tourists to the neighborhood. The museum on its ground floor also regularly hosts tours for school and community groups.

The paint on the ground-floor walls is peeling, and several tour groups have expressed concern that the paint flakes may contain lead or other toxic chemicals. In the last year, at least two groups have cancelled visits because of this concern.

The Roseway Cottage Board of Directors (RCBD) wants to repaint the four ground floor rooms using nontoxic paints derived from environmentally friendly, sustainable sources.

Benefits of Repainting

Refreshing the paint in the downstairs rooms will ensure that no more tours are cancelled due to health and safety reasons. It will also protect the fragile plaster walls, which are at risk of deteriorating when exposed to the air. Additionally, this update to the property will enable the Cottage to showcase images of its interior on its new website, which is its main promotional tool for attracting visitors.

Paint Choice

Five years ago, the RCBD repainted the upstairs rooms (currently used as office space) using a chalk-based paint manufactured by Greenway. While the paint was economically priced, it faded very quickly, so the RCBD is seeking an alternative product for the downstairs rooms.

Besides chalk, the most common bases for non-toxic paints are plant oils, milk, and beeswax. The RCBD has chosen a beeswax product, Beez-Kneez Eggshell, because it offers the following advantages:

- Least likely to fade—Beeswax hues normally keep their intensity two to three times as long as chalk-based paint and twice as long as paints based on plant oils or milk.
- Low fumes—While other non-toxic paints off-gas a mineral-smelling odor, beeswax paint emits on a slight smell, similar to the fragrance from a beeswax candle.
- Greatest resistance to scratches and scuffs—A matte beeswax paint compares in durability to a high-gloss paint based on chalk, plant oil, or milk. In a high-gloss product, a beeswax paint matches the durability of a conventional paint that includes toxic ingredients.

Proposed Painting Company

Ralph Roy and Sons Painting Company is a well-established Milltown business that has been operating since 1997. Ralph and his crew were the first painters in the local area to use nontoxic paints; they were also the first painting company in Connecticut to become certified through the Green Business Bureau (GBB).

Showing the significance of the cottage to the community positions the proposal as important.

A descriptive heading is more useful than a generic heading, such as "Background" or "Introduction."

Mentioning the cancellations shows that the situation is serious and urgent.

Headings make the proposal easy to skim and easy for stakeholders with varying interests to navigate. For instance, someone in search of financial information can skip over the preliminary content and go straight to the "Funding request" section below.

This proposal leads with results. The introduction spells out the specific benefits that repainting the rooms will generate so the readers can visualize the future state.

Here's the solution the RCBD has already tried.

Bulleted points enhance readability.

Here, the author could have provided a "tell-all" comparative analysis of the four different kinds of paints mentioned. But in the end, all the readers will want to know is why beeswax has been chosen.

This section emphasizes how closely the proposed work aligns with the granting organization's commitment to sustainability.

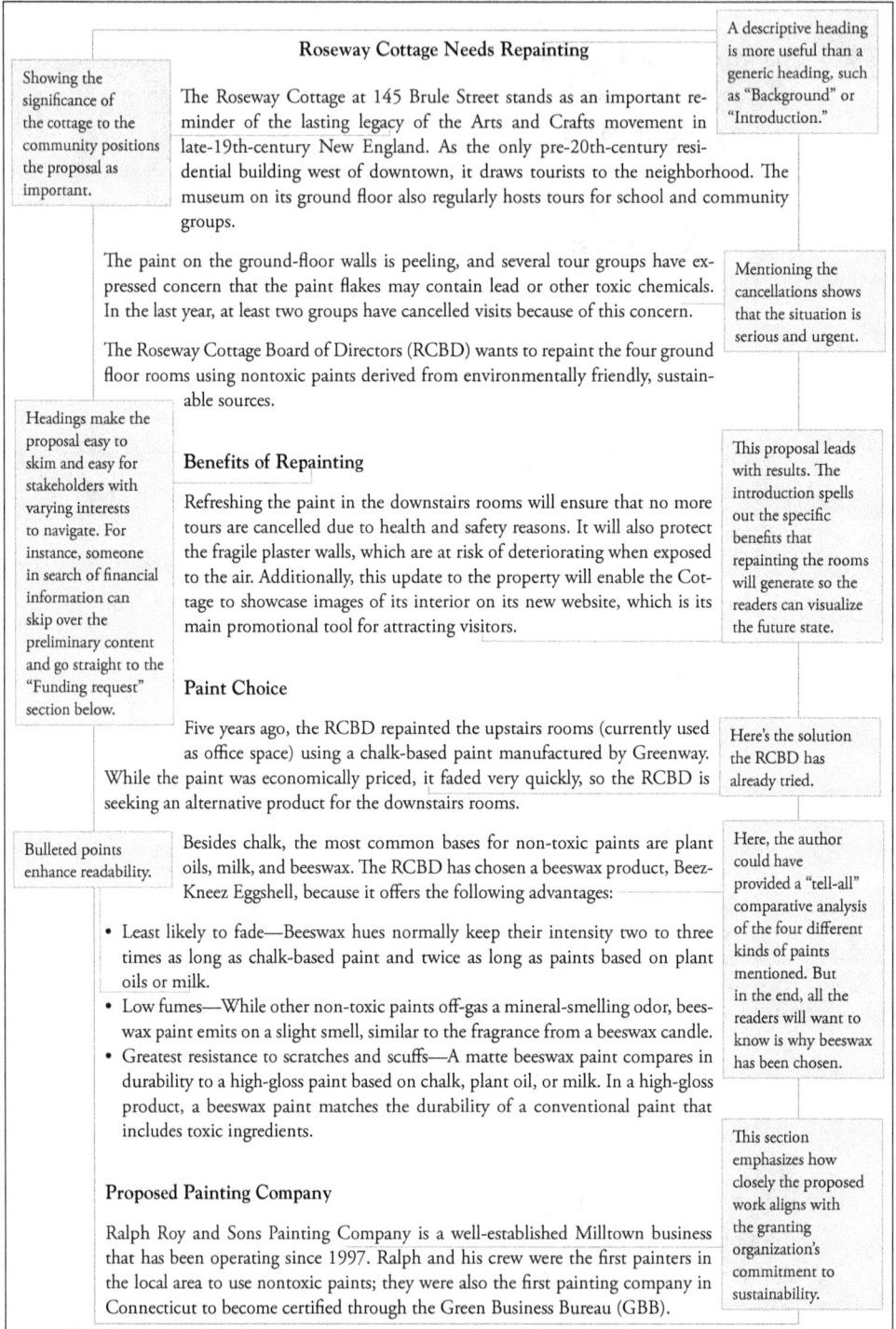

Figure 7.1 Proposal for a Heritage Society Restoration Grant

The GBB certification reflects Ralph's commitment to using sustainably sourced products and to operating his business according to sustainable principles. For example, Ralph's fleet of three lightweight trucks runs on ethanol, his office lights are solar-powered, and he provides electronic invoices and receipts.

Funding Request

The RCBD is requesting $1,425 (tax included) to repaint the four ground-floor rooms in nontoxic, beeswax-based paint. This amount will cover:

- 4 gallons of BeezKneez nontoxic primer
- 8 gallons of BeezKneez nontoxic matte paint in ochre yellow (current wall color)
- 2 gallons of BeezKneez nontoxic high-gloss paint (for wood trim)
- Site preparation, priming, and painting (2 coats) provided by Ralph Roy and Sons Painting Company

> Specific language describes the impact of the choice in concrete terms.

Because BeezKneez is a premium beeswax product, it costs about 20 percent more than the chalk-based paint that was used 5 years ago. However, it lasts about 30 percent longer than the average non-toxic paint, so the upfront investment will pay for itself in saved paint and labor costs down the road.

> The proposal anticipates an objection—a high price tag—and explains it away.

Project Schedule

Ralph Roy and Sons can begin work as soon as funding is granted, as early as the first week of April. It will take two to three days to complete:

- One day for site preparation, including washing, crack-filling, and sanding the walls
- One to two days for painting

> For a more complex project, the proposal would include a detailed breakdown of the timeline, roles, and responsibilities.

Ideally, the painting would be complete by the Memorial Day weekend, when the Cottage normally receives the first influx of summer tourists.

Contact Information
Stan Simmons
Chair, Rose Cottage Board of Directors
145 Brule St.
Milltown, CT 06055

Figure 7.1 (Continued)

Checklist for Grant Applications and Proposals

❑ Builds on relationships developed off-page

❑ Meets technical and formatting specifications outlined in the application form or RFP (if applicable)

❑ Describes, empathetically, the specific problem the proposal addresses

❑ Summarizes how the audience has tried to solve the problem (the Dr. Phil move)

❑ Frames the solution to align with the audience's interests and expectations

❑ Sells a vision that appeals to multiple stakeholders, including the Decision-maker, Secondary Readers, and Influencers

❑ Emphasizes the particular aspects of the solution that are relevant to the audience and omits irrelevant information (avoiding "tell-all" syndrome)

❑ Provides multiple pathways through the document

❑ Clearly and vividly contrasts the present state with the future state

  ○ Identifies near the beginning of the proposal the specific, concrete results the proposed product or service will produce

  ○ Uses concrete language to make the vision of the future real

  ○ Aligns specific parts of the solution with specific parts of the problem

  ○ Articulates the positive impact

  ○ States what to expect (how the project will unfold or how the product will be delivered and installed)

❑ Includes contact information of the person submitting the proposal

❑ Ends with a strong conclusion (perhaps looking ahead to the next conversation or action step)

CHAPTER 8

Pitch Decks

In 2018, Janet Bannister, a partner at the Toronto-based venture capital firm Real Ventures, reviewed 500 businesses. She invested in two.

Those numbers represent the typical odds you face if you're seeking venture capital (VC) funding. VC firms receive so many applications that you have just the blink of an eye to make a positive first impression and show the predictors of success that reviewers want to see.

Those key factors may not be what you expect, as venture capitalists bring a unique lens to investment opportunities. Unlike bankers, they're not looking for a solid track record in the market, steady cash flow, and a predictable path to a modest ROI. Instead, they're looking for a company that shows signs of being able to win big by innovating, responding to market needs, and adapting. Normally, a VC firm won't consider backing any business that doesn't show the potential to generate more than a billion dollars in revenue within a few years.

If you're seeking VC funding, your main communication tool will be a pitch deck, a brief slide presentation that busy VCs can review quickly. The job of a pitch deck is not to sell VCs on the business opportunity; the aim is to pique VCs' interest so you can get an in-person meeting with them. If you make it to that meeting, you'll then have the chance to present more detailed information about your company, through another slide deck or a short business plan.

Even if you're not pursuing VC funds, you'll find a pitch deck a useful item to add to your portfolio of business documents. It's a flexible tool that can be tailored to different investor audiences, such as angels and panels of pitch competitions. And because a pitch deck forces you to distill your value proposition down to its concise essence, developing one can help sharpen your overall strategic thinking about your company.

In this chapter, you'll learn how to choose the right format for your pitch deck, connect with your audience so you'll pique their interest, and answer three critical questions VCs want to see answered. I'll also introduce you to a four-part structure that will help you deliver a tight, persuasive message and share some tips for maximizing the visual impact of your slides.

Start by Choosing the Right Format

You already know the form your pitch deck will take—a slide presentation created in a program such as PowerPoint or Keynote. But how will you format your content within the deck?

The critical question here is whether your pitch needs to function as a standalone document, which readers will view without any live commentary from you, or as a visual aid to an oral presentation. These two situations require very different formatting.

Option 1: The Standalone Deck

If you're creating a standalone deck, then you'll need to create a template that allows space for ample text. As we'll see, your pitch deck should rely heavily on visuals, especially charts depicting your market analysis and financial projections. But if you won't be present to interpret those visuals, then you'll need to supply writing to do that for you.

That doesn't mean cramming 24-point text into a standard slide layout. Keep in mind that conventional slide formats, such as you'll find in PowerPoint's ready-made "themes," are designed for presentations that will be projected onto a large screen. Since your deck will be viewed in hard copy or on a computer screen, you can break the standard mold and create a new format. For your purposes, an 11- or 12-point font size should work well, and you can combine short blocks or columns of text with visuals.

Nancy Duarte, an authority on designing compelling slide presentation, has coined a new term for the standalone slide deck: Slidedoc®. In a Slidedoc, visuals and text work together seamlessly to present one main message per page. The goal is to create "short, atomic bites of content" that convey complex ideas, generate enthusiasm, and are easy to share.

As Duarte says, "Great slides spread,"[1] and you certainly want your pitch slides to spread the news about the fabulous investment opportunity your business offers.

Large professional services firms have been creating Slidedocs for years (without calling them that), so if anyone on your team has a consulting background, they should be well-equipped to help you prepare a pitch deck. You might also want to check out the free resources on Duarte's Slidedocs site (https://www.duarte.com/slidedocs/), including her PowerPoint template.

Option 2: Deck for a Live Presentation

If you're creating a deck for a live presentation, such as a pitch competition, you'll need to answer a couple of questions before you decide on the best format for your slides:

- **How large a room will you be presenting in?**
  The larger the room, the larger your font will need to be. For a boardroom, you can probably get away with 20-point text, maybe 18-point at a pinch. For a bigger room or an auditorium, you'll need at least 22-point font, larger if possible.
- **Will the deck circulate to people who haven't attended the live presentation?**
  When a deck must function as a visual aid to your live presentation and as a standalone document, then you face the awkward situation of serving two masters at once. Keep your font large enough for projection (minimum of 20 points) and make your slide headlines full sentences so that your key messages come across explicitly. You may also want to extend the number of slides in your deck so that you give yourself more room for text, without overwhelming your visuals, which should play the starring role in your presentation. (More slides shouldn't result in a longer presentation; you'll just spend less time displaying and commenting on each slide.)

---

[1] N. Duarte. *Slidedocs: Spread Ideas with Effective Visual Documents* (Santa Clara, CA: Duarte Inc., 2014), p. 4.

Learn How to Connect with Your Audience

In baseball, a great pitcher throws the ball so the batter will miss it. A perfect pitch sails across home plate at a speed or with a spin that perplexes the batter and makes it hard for them to connect bat to ball. In business, however, pitching is all about connecting. A successful pitch syncs with the audience's interests and convinces them that investing in the business will enable them to hit a home run. It enables them to visualize phenomenal success, for you and for them.

Your challenge, then, is to position the investment opportunity so that it resonates with your particular audience of investors. As you size up your audience, here are some questions to consider.

- What industries does the investor specialize in? (The term "investor" could refer to an individual, as in a single angel investor, or a group of people, such as a VC firm or pitch competition panel.)
- At what stage of a business's growth does the investor typically invest?
- What size of investment does the investor typically make?
- What companies has the investor backed in the past? What do these investments tell you about their personal interests and values? What do they look for in an investment opportunity?

At Real Ventures, Janet Bannister frequently receives pitch decks from businesses that aren't really "venture-backable." Since the firm invests in startups they believe can be worth hundreds of millions of dollars, a business that's likely to generate only a few millions in revenue doesn't even qualify to enter their ballpark. Do your homework so you know who you're playing ball with, what their expectations are, and how you can throw the ball so they'll want to swing for it with all their might.

You can tap into various resources to do this research:

- Websites of VC firms, which usually feature a list of companies they've funded and bios of the partners making the investment decisions.
- LinkedIn profiles of individual investors.
- Media coverage of individual investors.

- Insights from people in your network who have interacted with the investor.
- Interviews with companies that have received funding from the investor.
- Media coverage of companies that have received funding from the investor.

Because it takes a lot of effort to prepare a pitch deck, you might be tempted to use the same deck with multiple audiences. That's the quickest way to kick yourself right out of the ballgame. Yes, the "facts" of your business remain constant, but numbers don't speak for themselves. The way you frame the opportunity for each particular investment audience provides context that can make or break a deal.

Focus on Three Critical Questions

A successful pitch answers three critical questions:

1. What is your business?
2. Why will you succeed?
3. What will the ROI be?

Sounds simple, doesn't it? But when you delve into those questions, each of them opens up into further questions that require extensive thought and analysis. Before you can answer the three critical questions concisely in pitch form, you'll need to spend some time exploring them in detail. Only once you've plumbed their depths will you be able to select the most compelling ideas and data and weave them together into a persuasive message for investors.

1. What Is Your Business?

This question invites you to dig into why you started your company and how your offerings fit into the landscape of your industry:

- What market need sparked the idea for your company?
- What business or socioeconomic trends does your business align with?

- Who are your customers, and what problem do you solve for them?
- What products or services do you provide?
- What is your value proposition?
- What is your business model? (How do you profit from your products or services?)
- How do you adapt to market demand? (How do you develop your products or services, test them in the market, and adapt accordingly?)
- Who are the members of your team?

For startups, the last two questions can hold a lot of sway with investors. When she's evaluating a pitch, Janet wants to see evidence that the company is able to nimbly iterate and pivot. She explains: "I often look at how quickly a team can learn, revise, test it again, and go through that cycle of testing and learning and iterating. How quickly they go through that cycle is very important."

Because startups can't refer to a long track record to establish their credibility, the profile of the founding team can also exert a strong influence on the investment decision. What expertise and what character traits make your team all-stars on their playing field? What in their past experience predicts that they'll have the agility, resourcefulness, and tenacity to take a company from zero to a billion dollars within just a few years? How can the investors trust that you and your team are the best people to spend their money?

2. Why Will You Succeed?

Answering the first critical question involves description, but answering the second question requires you to construct a logical argument. This is a key distinction, which many pitchers overlook.

While you may see the "evidence" pointing toward your success as incontrovertible "facts," any statement you make about the future is debatable. To convince your audience that your data and assumptions are valid, you'll need to think through the following questions in depth:

- What business or socioeconomic trends will help you succeed?
- How are people currently solving the problem that you can help them solve?

- What evidence do you have that customers want what you have to offer?
- What traction have you gained in the market?
- Who are your competitors inside your industry? Outside your industry?
- What are you offering that's different from and better than what your competitors offer?
- What new competitors can you imagine entering your market? How will you defend yourself against that threat?
- Who else has tried what you're trying to do, and why have they failed? How will you mitigate against the risks that overcame the companies that flopped?

One of the biggest oversights Janet notices in pitch decks is the lack of a thorough competitive analysis. "It's amazing to me how many pitches I see that don't go into in-depth on the competitive analysis," she says. It's especially important, she says, to consider who else could enter the market. Maybe you're swimming in a blue ocean now, but it's sure to become red soon. How will you protect yourself against future competitors? A patent application will not likely be enough to sway investors because someone else could solve the same problem you're solving for your customers in another way. What kind of a "competitive moat" have you created that will make it hard for other companies to keep up with you?

3. What Will the ROI Be?

This question requires you to present detailed financial projections, based on well-founded assumptions. As you present your projections, watch out for these five common mistakes that turn off investors:

- **Mistake #1: Downplaying the risk.** Your audience isn't looking for a risk-free investment opportunity because that doesn't exist. Instead, they're looking for an opportunity that will balance calculated risk with expected reward; the greater the reward, the greater the risk will likely be. Show that you've assessed all possible risks and have strategies in place to overcome them should they arise.

- **Mistake #2: Underestimating the timeline.** New York-based VC Taylor Davidson recommends assuming that it will take you twice the amount of time and money you initially estimate to achieve your milestones.[2]
- **Mistake #3: Assuming the numbers will speak for themselves.** Explicitly state the key points your graphs and charts are meant to make. Don't leave it up to your audience to do the work of interpreting the financial data you present as they may not hear the numbers saying the same things you do.
- **Mistake #4: Leaving the customer out of the picture.** Yes, it's important to document the size of your market, but it's equally important to show exactly how you'll get customers. Consider such questions as these:
  - What will it cost you to acquire customers?
  - How do you know customers will be willing and able to buy your solution?
  - What will the lifetime value (LTV) of a customer be?
- **Mistake #5: Omitting a spending plan.** Investors want to see how you'll use the money you're requesting. Early on in a conversation with an investor, you may not be able to list specific amounts, but you can still give ranges or proportions to show how an infusion of capital will support specific business activities. As Michael Porter has so succinctly put it, "The essence of strategy is choosing to perform activities differently than rivals do."[3] So which activities will the requested funding enable you to perform?

Once you've thoroughly explored the questions beneath each of the three critical questions listed above, then you're ready to articulate key points that will resonate the most strongly with your target audience. It's time to start building your deck.

---

[2]T. Davidson. n.d. "How to Pitch Your Financial Projections," *Foresight website*, https://foresight.is/learn/presenting-financials, (accessed October 10, 2019).
[3]M. Porter. 1996. "What Is Strategy," *Harvard Business Review* 74, no. 6, pp. 61–78.

Structure Your Deck

A 2019 study conducted by Harvard professor Tom Eisenmann and DocSend, a company that provides document sharing and tracking services, found that the average investor spends just 3 minutes and 44 seconds reviewing a pitch deck. The study, which analyzed 200 pitch decks that successfully attracted seed funding, also found that the average deck included just 19 slides.[4]

The study's authors recommend, therefore, that pitchers keep their decks to 20 slides or less. This cap on deck length doesn't allow you much space in which to address the three critical questions investors want you to answer. So you'll need to make some strategic decisions about what to include and what to leave out.

The following diagram should simplify that decision process. It shows the 10 essential topics the DocSend study recommends a pitch deck cover. Because the human brain processes information best when it's grouped into broad categories and then broken down, I've organized DocSend's linear sequence into four main topics, with each topic including at least one subsection (Figure 8.1).

Notice how the 10 topics are arranged to take the audience on a journey, starting with an overview of the opportunity and drilling deeper and deeper into detail. As you build your deck, keep that overview-to-details structure in mind, repeating it as your document unfolds. As you introduce each of the four sections, give a high-level summary of the section's main point. (You may want to use a part-divider slide to do this.) Then, as you develop that point by examining specific details, connect each supporting idea or data set back to that overview statement.

Notice the role that emotion plays in the audience journey you're creating. Your deck needs to start by generating strong emotional resonance; you must "hook" the reader emotionally with a precise, vivid description of the problem you're solving and the solution you're offering. You must also produce a sense of urgency by addressing the question of "Why Now?" Only once you've captured your audience's attention by tugging on these emotional strings will you be able to interest them in the technical, operational, and financial aspects of the opportunity you're presenting.

[4]DocSend.n.d. "What We Learned from 200 Startups Who Raised $360M." https://docsend.com/view/p8jxsqr, (accessed October 10, 2019).

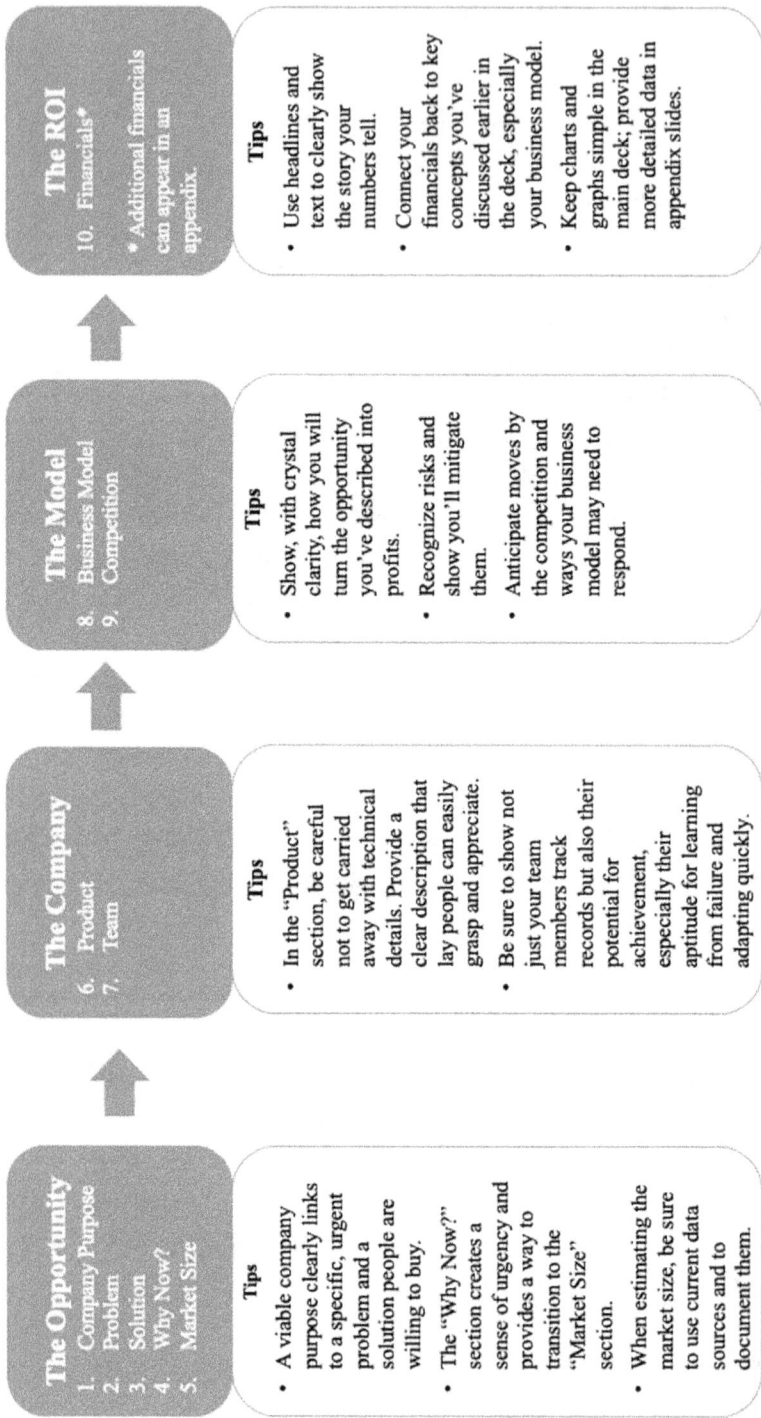

The Opportunity
1. Company Purpose
2. Problem
3. Solution
4. Why Now?
5. Market Size

Tips

- A viable company purpose clearly links to a specific, urgent problem and a solution people are willing to buy.

- The "Why Now?" section creates a sense of urgency and provides a way to transition to the "Market Size" section.

- When estimating the market size, be sure to use current data sources and to document them.

The Company
6. Product
7. Team

Tips

- In the "Product" section, be careful not to get carried away with technical details. Provide a clear description that lay people can easily grasp and appreciate.

- Be sure to show not just your team members track records but also their potential for achievement, especially their aptitude for learning from failure and adapting quickly.

The Model
8. Business Model
9. Competition

Tips

- Show, with crystal clarity, how you will turn the opportunity you've described into profits.

- Recognize risks and show you'll mitigate them.

- Anticipate moves by the competition and ways your business model may need to respond.

The ROI
10. Financials*

* Additional financials can appear in an appendix.

Tips

- Use headlines and text to clearly show the story your numbers tell.

- Connect your financials back to key concepts you've discussed earlier in the deck, especially your business model.

- Keep charts and graphs simple in the main deck; provide more detailed data in appendix slides.

Figure 8.1 Four-part structure for a pitch deck

Given that your deck should rely heavily on visuals to convey your ideas, you'll need to allow generous white space to show off your diagrams and charts. (Busy investors like Janet get impatient with decks with crammed layouts because they're too hard to read.) So you'll need to take a minimalist approach as you develop the content for each section. How do you decide which content should make it into your final, ultra-trim deck? The following pointers should help:

- **Aim for depth rather than breadth.** Within each of your deck's 10 subsections, concentrate on communicating just a few well-supported ideas. For example, it's better to provide three reasons you'll outrun the competition, backed up by solid evidence, than six unsubstantiated reasons.

- **Keep your overall goal in mind.** Wooing an investor takes time and usually involves several conversations, so be mindful of where you are in the process. In many situations, the aim of a pitch deck is simply to persuade your audience to invest time in a live meeting with you. ("Convince me that your idea is worth me carving an hour out of my schedule," says Janet.) In such a case, concentrate on presenting the most essential ideas and data, while indicating that there's more where they came from.

- **Craft a compelling story.** As you consider what ideas and information to include, choose those pieces of content that fit together to form The Story of Our Shared Success. Part of that story could include your company history, how your product or service came to be, and what you've achieved so far. But that's just background to the exciting narrative you want your audience to envision— your journey together from where you are now to astonishing financial success.

  Emphasizing the story elements of your deck should help you avoid the common pitfall of failing to recognize the competition. All great plots are driven by struggle, as the hero contests against forces of nature, other people, and their own personal limitations. The more accurately you paint the picture of how your business will grapple with the real challenges it faces—and adapt as necessary— the more effectively it will draw your audience into the narrative.

A Simple Method for Conquering Writing Overwhelm

A pitch deck operates on a kind of paradox: it must present deep, complex thinking in simple, ultra-concise language and visuals. Navigating this challenge can cause feelings of overwhelm, even writer's block. To cope, many writers make the tactical error of trying to produce a lean document from the beginning, an approach that tends to lead to surface-level thinking and data-starved arguments.

In one of my favorite books on writing, *Writing to Change the World*, Mary Pipher describes an "accordion method"[1] that works well when you're trying to develop ideas *and* express those ideas with great clarity and focus. Here's how it works:

1. **Fill the accordion with air.** Start by writing expansively—include all the detailed information you think might be useful to your audience. You might do this by creating rough slides, by writing notes by hand, or by drafting a long-form document in a word processing program.
2. **Squeeze the accordion.** Pare back your writing to make it as spare as you can. Contract each section of your deck or document to make it as lean as possible.
3. **Open up the accordion again.** Reread your writing and add in any details you think would strengthen it.
4. **If you need to, squeeze the accordion again**, and repeat the open-squeeze cycle as many times as required until you've created a document that's comprehensive and clear as well as focused and concise.

[1] M. Pipher. 2006. *Writing to Change the World* (New York, NY: Penguin), Chapter 8, Kindle.

Make a Strong Visual Impact

Whether you're working in a slidedoc format or developing a pitch deck that will be projected on a large screen, each slide should center on a compelling visual. And the meaning of that visual must meet two exacting criteria. It must be crystal clear and aligned directly with the slide's key message. When a visual fails to pass one or both of these tests, reader confusion results. And the worst possible thing you can do, other than bore a potential investor, is to confuse them!

Table 8.1 lists six common issues that show up in poorly designed visuals and ways to fix them. You can use this list as a trouble-shooting guide as you examine the graphic design of your slides for possible flaws. In particular, keep your eyes open for irrelevant visuals that don't support the slide headline; Figure 8.2 illustrates this problem, which is much more common than you might think.

Get Feedback on Your Pitch before You Pitch It!

Because they must present complex ideas so concisely, and because they rely heavily on elements of graphic design, pitch decks present one of the toughest writing challenges you'll face as an entrepreneur. For that reason, I recommend sharing your draft deck with as many trusted readers as you can.

"Trusted readers" should, of course, be people with whom you can safely share highly confidential information about your company. They should also be folks who either have experience communicating with investors (the ideal) or can role-play an investor audience. As we've seen, investors approach a deck with particular interests and questions, and relevant feedback needs to take that unique perspective into account.

As you invite others to critique your deck, you may want to request comments on particular aspects of it. Sometimes the best way to get relevant feedback is to ask reviewers specific questions about parts of your deck you sense may be unclear or a bit wobbly (undersupported).

If at first you don't land funds with your pitch deck, be sure to ask for feedback on it—and incorporate that feedback into your next version. In the study mentioned earlier in this chapter, most of the companies succeeded in raising seed funding after contacting 20 to 30 different investors. Learn as much as you can from each investor you approach so you can iterate your way to success.

Table 8.1 Common design flaws in pitch decks

Design issue	Why it's a problem	How to fix it
Poor legibility due to small font size or crowding	Readers don't want to squint. They'd rather just discard your deck. Keep in mind that not all your readers will have perfect vision.	For slidedoc decks, use a font size of 11 or 12 points. For projected decks, use a font of at least 20 points, preferably 24. Also allow generous white space around visuals and chunks of text.
Missing or unclear labels	Without a title, it's hard to tell what story the visual is meant to convey. If a graph is missing axis labels (or if those labels are ambiguous), its meaning may escape the reader altogether.	Give each visual a title summarizing its meaning. For graphs, clearly label each axis, including units of measurement (if applicable).
Wrong choice of visual for the story the data is meant to tell	Charts are not interchangeable. Each type of chart suits a different kind of data story. For example, if you want to show a trend over time, a line graph will do that well, but a bar chart or table won't really work.	For help choosing the best chart for a given data set, check out the data visualization classic *Show Me the Numbers: Designing Tables and Graphs to Enlighten* by Stephen Few.
Weak or illogical connection with the slide's key message	The most stunning visual will flop if it doesn't connect directly and obviously to the slide's key message. Each of your slides should articulate a single key message through its headline, and the slide visuals should function as evidence to support that message.[1] See Figure 8.2, an example of a slide containing irrelevant content that misaligns with the slide headline.	Resist the urge to include a visual just because it contains great data or looks amazing. Link your visuals to your key message by providing clear labels and, if necessary, interpretive text. "Interpretive text" could include a sentence introducing a visual, a detailed caption summarizing the visual's meaning, or a text box or paragraph explaining the point the visual makes.

[1] Pennsylvania State University professor Michael Alley has conducted studies showing that the "assertion–evidence" (AE) approach to slide design, which uses full sentences for headlines, results in greater reader comprehension than an approach that relies on topic headlines. Check out our AE tutorials and templates at assertion-evidence.com.

Table 8.1 Continued

Design issue	Why it's a problem	How to fix it
Too many colors and/ or details	Your readers will assume that each color, arrow, asterisk, line, and icon you include in your visual conveys a specific meaning. If your color scheme or other elements of your visual create too much complexity, the reader will feel overwhelmed and confused.	Keep it simple. Use no more than five colors in a visual and limit the use of graphic elements that don't really add value to the visual.
Contradiction of standard visual conventions	Many elements of graphic design carry conventional meanings. For instance, a square conveys clear definition and boundaries. An arrow pointing to the right indicates some sort of linear progress. In Western cultures, the color red signifies danger (while in some Eastern cultures, it signifies good luck). When you use a visual element in a way that contradicts its usual meaning, you baffle your readers. For instance, if you describe your solution as "holistic" but represent its component parts as four triangles forming a pyramid, readers might have trouble grasping the inclusive, integrative nature of your offering. Circles offer a more culturally standard way of representing wholeness, whereas pyramids tend to show some kind of a hierarchy.	For every diagram you create to represent a concept, challenge yourself to imagine an alternative design. Which option feels most intuitive to you? How does the design use the elements of shape and color to reinforce the idea or ideas you're trying to convey? If you find such questions tough to tackle, you may want to brush up on what Guenther Kress and Theo van Leeuwen call "the grammar of visual design."[2] Here are a few books I recommend: • *Universal Principles of Design* by William Lidwell, Kritina Holden, and Jill Butler • *The Non-designer's Design Book* by Robin Williams • *The Design of Everyday Things* by Donald Norman

<hr>

[2] G. Kress and T. van Leeuwen. 1996. *Reading Images: The Grammar of Visual Design* (New York, NY: Routledge).

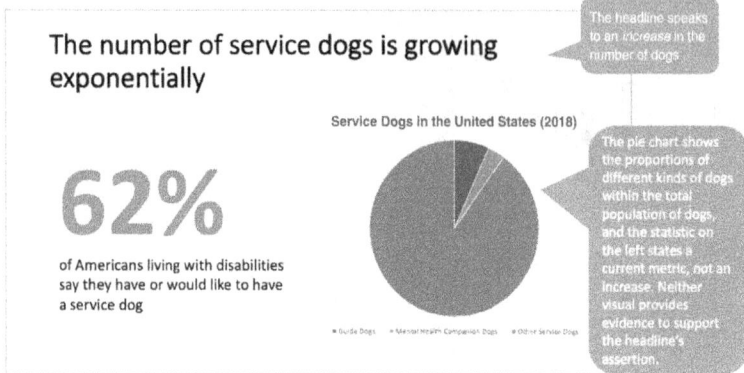

Figure 8.2 Slide with an irrelevant visual

Where to Find Examples of Successful Pitch Decks

The best examples are pitch decks that have been successfully used with the particular investor or VC firm you're targeting. Pitch competitions often post winning decks, and you may also find online sample decks from companies that have secured funding from a particular firm. (Try searching for slide presentations by a company that's recently finished a funding round. While the company won't likely post the complete pitch deck online, they may be using parts of the deck—minus the confidential financial information—as marketing collateral.)

A great source of pitch decks, along with video commentaries, is Slidebean's repository of famous pitches at https://pitchdeckexamples. com. (Slidebean offers AI-powered slide design services for entrepreneurs seeking funding.) Check out one of my favorites, the Airbnb pitch deck, redesigned by Slidebean to give it a contemporary look and feel: https://pitchdeckexamples.com/startups/airbnb-pitch-deck.

Of course, the best way to learn about what works and doesn't work in a pitch deck is to test out your document on a real audience. Keep an eye out for opportunities to participate in pitch competitions, and don't be shy about asking the judges for specific feedback to help you improve your presentation.

Checklist for a Pitch Deck

❑ Uses the appropriate format (standalone deck or deck for live presentation)
❑ Frames the content to connect with the audience:
  ○ What industries does the investor specialize in?
  ○ At what stage of a business's growth does the investor typically invest?
  ○ What size of investment does the investor typically make?
  ○ What companies has the investor backed in the past? What do these investments tell you about their personal interests and values? About what they look for in an investment opportunity?
❑ Provides well-supported answers to the three critical questions:
  ○ What is your business?
  ○ Why will you succeed?
  ○ What will the ROI be?
❑ Covers the 10 essential topics:
  ○ The Opportunity—Company Purpose, Problem, Solution, Why Now? and market Size
  ○ The Company—Product and Team
  ○ The Model—Business Model and Competition
  ○ The ROI—Financials
❑ Creates an audience journey that forms The Story of Our Shared Success
❑ Anticipates possible questions and objections and supplies answers to them
❑ Recognizes risks and provides ways to mitigate them
❑ Provides financial projections, including text that interprets the numbers
❑ Includes detailed financials in an appendix
❑ Makes a strong visual impact through spacious slide layouts and relevant, well-labeled charts and diagrams

CHAPTER 9

Business Plans

Is the traditional business plan dead? Maybe. At least some of the conventional assumptions about this classic piece of business writing need to die.

If you're seeking a conventional loan or a contribution from an angel investor, then you'll certainly need some kind of document to show the value of the investment opportunity you're offering. But exactly what that document should look like varies greatly from business to business and investor to investor.

In this chapter, we'll focus on business plan requirements for banks, but many of the insights apply to angel investors as well. Although templates for business plans abound, you'll discover that there's really no one-size-fits-all structure for an effective business plan. Like all the other types of writing we've explored so far, a business plan performs best when it caters to the particular interests of the target audience.

So if you're not going to get a template from this chapter, what will you take from it? You'll learn what a business plan is and what it isn't so you can shape a document tailored to your lender. You'll also learn how to create a logical argument, a compelling business case, and a concise executive summary of your plan.

The Purpose of a Business Plan

As a manager in the Commercial Banking division of CIBC (the Canadian Imperial Bank of Commerce), Kyle Rogers spends a lot of his time paging through business plans from a wide range of industries. His client list includes businesses to which the bank has loaned between about 1 and 5 million dollars.

For him, the business plan is a tool that needs to answer three key questions:

- What is the opportunity?
- Why is it significant?
- How will the business pay the bank back?

Ideally, the plan provides focused, well-supported answers to each of those queries—without drowning the reader in irrelevant details.

In Kyle's experience, a five page business plan can outshine a 20-, 50-, or even 100-page document. Kyle wants to be able to access key information quickly, not root through volumes of unnecessary background. In fact, excessive length can kill a plan's success.

"We don't need to know the business as well as the business owner," Kyle explains. What's needed? "A smaller number of pages and more thoughtful analysis."

Kyle recommends that entrepreneurs sit down with the lender as early in the application process as possible. "It's never too early to meet," he says. An early conversation allows you to figure out exactly what information the bank will be looking for in a plan, based on the state of the business, the industry, and other factors. With this input, you can then create a brief, customized plan addressing the precise points that will make or break your case.

Kyle shakes his head over applicants who go to great effort, and sometimes great expense, developing beefy business plans that completely miss the mark. For instance, he recalls one applicant who assembled pages of in-depth documentation to verify a contract with a major client. In the end, all that paper work did nothing to further the applicant's case. In fact, it pointed up a major risk: most of the applicant's business depended on the single (well-documented) client. Instead of describing all the ins and outs of his relationship with his major client, the applicant should have presented a risk mitigation plan showing how his business could cope with the sudden loss of that client.

The real job of a business plan is to present a compelling analysis of your business numbers, showing that the business will make enough money to pay back the loan, on schedule. The sooner you're able to meet with the bank to share some background about your business and your initial financial projections, the better equipped you and your accountant will be to answer potential objections and wave away any red flags the bank perceives. Starting the lending process with a conversation enables you to get to know your audience so you can attune your writing to their needs, interests, and biases rather than simply filling out a template that may or may not suit your readers or your situation.

Understand What a Business Plan Isn't

The name "business plan" creates the misleading impression that the document's job is to describe or explain how your business will operate. If you're creating a business plan for internal purposes, then it will indeed function as a conventional plan, providing a road map for you and your team to follow. But a business plan written for a lender actually plays a different role. As we've seen, it must show why and how your business will succeed. It must present a persuasive argument, building a convincing business case.

A business case differs from a "business story," which is a term we hear a lot these days, so much so that it's turned into a jargon term. People use "story" or "storytelling" to describe the structure of pitches, proposals, analytical reports, and various other kinds of documents, business plans among them. But that widespread labeling can prove misleading, especially in the case of business plans. A persuasive business plan includes some elements of narrative, but its overarching form must follow the logical structure of argumentative writing.

If you want to construct a compelling business case, you must put story in its proper place. Story can show how your company has evolved into its current state, and as in a pitch deck, it can enable readers to imagine your future success. But within the context of a business case, story supplements a persuasive argument; it doesn't carry the main weight.

It's important to recognize the difference between story and argument because the two modes of writing follow two different structures. A story presents a series of events, starting with an initial problem and then developing through a string of escalating incidents until some sort of crisis happens, followed by a resolution. Its linear structure looks like the one in Figure 9.1.

An argument, on the other hand, logically leads the reader to accept a certain truth, based on a set of claims backed up by credible evidence. An

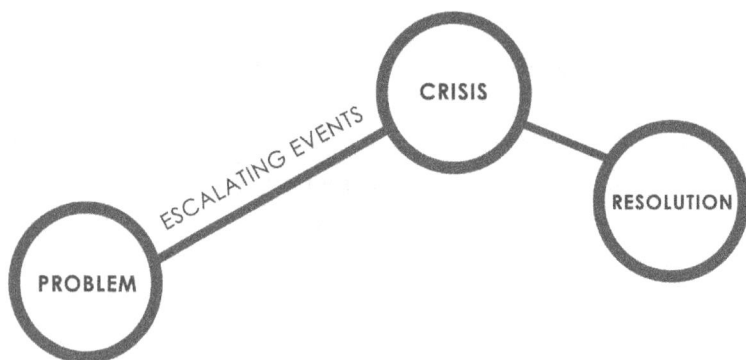

Figure 9.1 Story structure

effective argument arranges ideas into a hierarchical structure rooted in a single main idea. It presents a set of closely related claims, backed up by pieces of credible evidence, and all of this information works together to show why the main idea is true.

In a business plan, you must convince your reader to accept one core idea, that your business will succeed and repay the lender on their investment. It's not enough for each concept and data point in your plan to relate to that idea, as in the loose structure of a narrative. Each bit of content in your plan must directly support and develop the core idea. The hierarchical structure of a business plan's argument looks like the one in Figure 9.2:

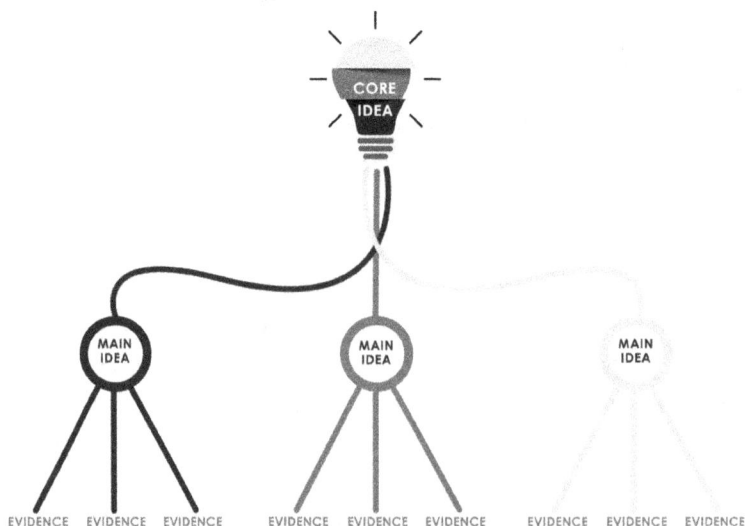

Figure 9.2 Argument structure of a business plan

How to Build a Watertight Argument

To construct a persuasive argument, start by crafting short responses (one or two sentences, or a few bullet points) to the three key questions lenders want you to answer:

- What is the opportunity?
- Why is it significant?
- How will the business pay the bank back?

Then, based on your preliminary conversations with the lender, identify additional questions you need to answer within those three broad categories. (The more directly you can echo the phrasing the lender has used to pose those questions, the better.) Write short answers to each of those questions, and note the evidence you'll use to back up your answer. That might include data from customer surveys or focus group, research into industry trends, case studies from companies similar to yours, and financial data your accountant has helped you prepare.

Now, you have the raw ingredients you need to start constructing an argument comprised of strong claims and credible evidence. Before you start writing, you might find it helpful to sketch a tree diagram similar to the example in Figure 9.3. I sometimes like to create a tree diagram from Post-it notes so that I can move claims and evidence around as I start to write.

As you draft your argument, be sure to logically connect your evidence to your claims. You must make the logical linkages explicit because leaving it up to your reader to "connect the dots" leaves your document open to the risk of misinterpretation.

For instance, let's say you're developing a business plan for a new app called Yip, which enables dog owners to locate dog-friendly spaces (stores, restaurants, and recreational facilities) near them. One thread of your argument points out that pet owners in their 20s and 30s don't want to leave their pets at home when they go shopping or enjoy time with friends. You have data from a recent PetSmart study confirming that 85 percent of dog owners under 35 would choose a dog-friendly store over a store that doesn't allow pets.

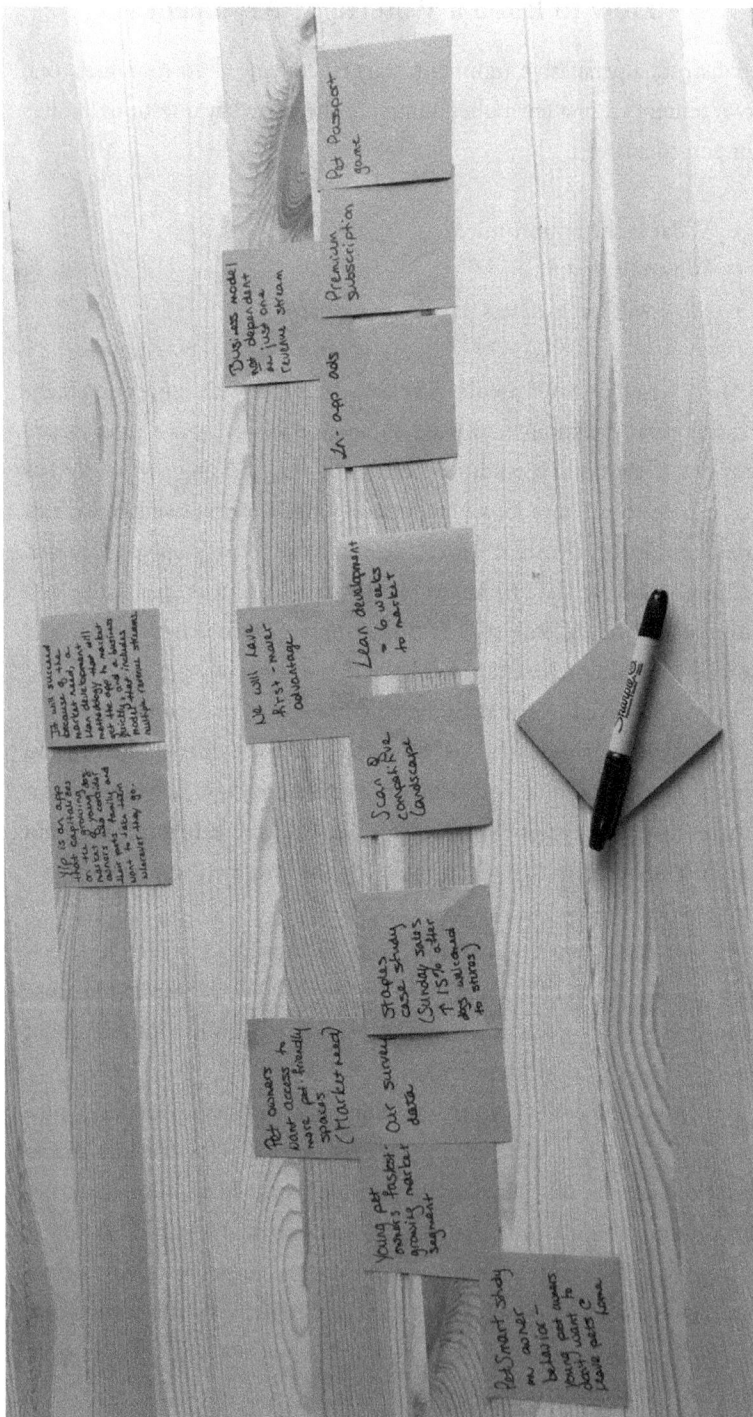

Figure 9.3 Business plan tree diagram in progress

This statistic could help support your claim that there's a market need for your app—but only if you provide a link between the data from the PetSmart study and the market trend of a growing number of young dog owners who enjoy spending money as well as time on their pets. If you can show that young dog owners form the largest and fastest-growing segment of the pet care market, for instance, then the data from the PetSmart study appears relevant. Figure 9.4 shows how such market trend information creates a logical link between the claim that there's a market need for Yip and the data documenting consumer behavior in the target market.

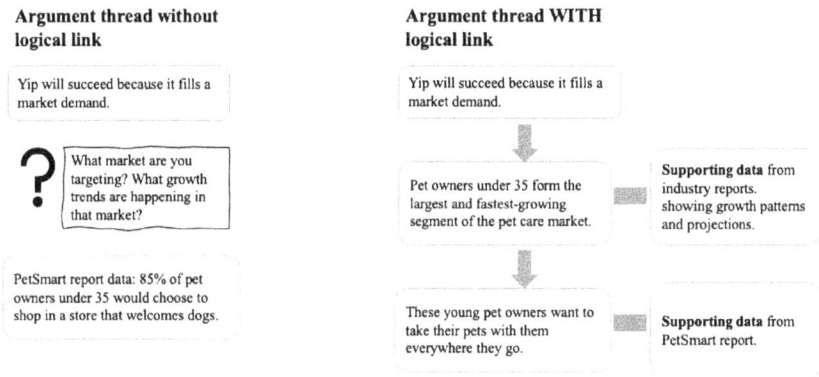

Argument thread without logical link

Yip will succeed because it fills a market demand.

? What market are you targeting? What growth trends are happening in that market?

PetSmart report data: 85% of pet owners under 35 would choose to shop in a store that welcomes dogs.

Argument thread WITH logical link

Yip will succeed because it fills a market demand.

Pet owners under 35 form the largest and fastest-growing segment of the pet care market.

Supporting data from industry reports. showing growth patterns and projections.

These young pet owners want to take their pets with them everywhere they go.

Supporting data from PetSmart report.

Figure 9.4 Logical link between a claim and supporting evidence

When presenting evidence to support your claims, practice viewing data sources through a skeptical lens. Be prepared to show why your sources are trustworthy and why their findings can be generalized. In the case of the PetSmart study, for example, you might want to mention how many stores and geographical areas it covered and what research methodology it used.

As with pitch decks, never assume that any kind of financial information you provide in a business plan, either in the body of the plan or in an appendix, can speak for itself. Take your reader by the hand and direct them to specific parts of your financial documentation that support your argument. In some cases, you might do that by providing a summary sentence or paragraph interpreting the financial data. In other cases, you might need to point the reader directly to a specific page or chart in your appendix.

Scrutinize Your Business Case

As the business founder, you're invested heart and soul in your venture, so it takes hard work to view it from an outside perspective. But the more skeptical a lens you can bring to your emerging plan, the stronger a case you'll be able to make.

Think of this as a trouble-shooting exercise in two phases. In the first phase, your aim is to verify that you've provided just the right amount of detail to allow the lender to make a positive decision. In the second phase, your goal is to anticipate possible objections so you can rebut them within the plan.

1. Providing the Right Amount of Detail

In Chapter 7, I advised against falling into "tell-all syndrome," the tendency to overwhelm the audience with information only tangentially relevant to the solution being offered. While this can be a hazard for business plan writers as well, a more common pitfall is to leave out critical information the lender needs to know in order to approve your funding request.

Table 9.1 lists the "standard" topics a traditional business plan covers. Depending on your situation, some of these topics will merit more attention than others. For instance, if you own a manufacturing business employing 40 people, then you may require a detailed operating plan. But if you run a three-person software development company, that section might be scant in your document.

Build up the sections that give you the best leverage for persuading your audience. If your business is new, for example, don't waste time trying to manufacture a detailed company history or overthink your financial forecast, which has no history to back up its assumptions. Instead, a more strategic approach would be to articulate a clear vision, demonstrate the market need, and play up your team's strengths.

Feel free to shuffle the order of topics and change conventional labels to suit your circumstances. As you develop the relationship with your lender, ask them for input regarding the topics and arrangement of topics. Kyle stresses that banks are usually happy to work with a business owner and their accountant "in partnership" throughout the application

Table 9.1 Traditional business plan topics

Section topic	Possible subtopics
Business overview	• Business purpose • Overview of products, services, and customer base • Industry background and trends • Economic and social trends • Regulatory environment
The market	• Target segment • Details of products and services • Competitive analysis • Market trends • Risks
Sales and marketing plan	• Business model • Revenue streams • Suppliers • Advertising and promotion • Pricing and distribution • Sales process • Customer service policies
Operating plan	• Business location • Lease details • Equipment • Technology • Environmental considerations
Human resources plan	• Key team members • Policies and procedures
Action plan	• Key milestones and activities • Timeline • Key metrics for measuring success
Financial plan	• Funding request • Historical financial performance • Projected financial performance • Income statement • Balance sheet • Cash flow sheet • Budget

process. If you're wondering whether the outline you have in mind will enable you to hit all the points your lender is hoping to see, why not ask?

2. Anticipating Objections

To succeed as an entrepreneur, you must be a visionary and an optimist. But lenders are trained pessimists, so to convince them your vision is viable, you must train yourself to anticipate and deflect their negative reactions.

As you draft your business plan, picture yourself presenting it to a crowd of hecklers who are questioning each point you make. Imagine them shouting out three comments over and over again:

- How do you know that's true?
- Where did you get that data from?
- So what?

Paying attention to those three heckler questions can help you anticipate the objections that will likely go through your lender's head as they read your completed plan.

If your "product" is something intangible, such as a software application or a technology that you haven't yet developed, then your business plan faces particular challenges. How do you convince pessimists of the value of something they can't see or touch or of something that hasn't even been invented?

Richard Howe works with Kyle at the CIBC as a manager of Commercial Banking specializing in the technology and innovation sector. He notices that many of the business plans he reads are "too descriptive and wishy-washy." "They don't drill down to what I want to see as a lender," he explains. "There's not enough substance."

"Substance" for an investor means evidence that there's market demand for what the business has to offer, solid financials, and proof that the intangible product will make a tangible impact. Let's say you're seeking funding for technology that enables a ship to navigate without disturbing marine life with sonar waves. The technology may function as an abstract concept in your lender's mind, but here are some ways you could make it concrete for them:

- **Show the market demand.** Refer to the market size, industry trends (including environmental policies), and data that show customers in your target market are investing in eco-friendly equipment.

- **Provide solid financials.** Richard looks for a clear, compelling "numbers story" that shows how the business will make money and pay the bank back.
- **Show the tangible impact. (Answer the question "So what?")** Describe how a ship's crew uses the technology and the observable benefits it brings, such as improved efficiency (navigation is automated), reduced fuel consumption, and a competitive advantage over ships with conventional navigation systems.

Buzzwords won't sway a lender, Richard warns. It takes hard data, especially detailed and realistic financial data, to make your business plan concrete and convincing. And don't overlook "data" from your biography and the biographies of your team members. When you're seeking funding for an innovative business idea that hasn't yet been proven, demonstrating your team's proven character can add significant weight to your argument.

Try This Instant Fix for Wordy Writing

A business plan is a "high-stakes document." Because a lot is riding on it, you may find yourself laboring over its style, trying to make the writing sound more formal and impressive than the writing you produce for more routine documents, such as team e-mails. Be careful: when you try too hard to sound smart and sophisticated, you can cause your style to become impersonal and bloated.

To create a style that's smart but trim, keep it personal. Rather than speaking about your company in the third person, use the more natural first person in its plural form. Rather than saying, "Blueberry was launched in October 2017 in response to a perceived market need for waterproof baby monitors," try a more conversational approach, speaking in your own voice: "We launched Blueberry in October 2017 because we noticed more and more parents were hunting for waterproof baby monitors."

See how much more energetic the second sentence sounds? It also sets up the development of the Blueberry as an intriguing story for you to develop. Where did you see parents "hunting" for next-generation monitors? How many of them were hunting? How desperate were they in their search?

As you concentrate on crafting a compelling written argument, remember that your business plan forms part of an ongoing conversation with the lender. The writing should sound like you (the smartest, most professional version of you) so that the way you present yourself in print continues to foster the rapport and trust you've been building in person.

Create a Compelling Executive Summary

In some ways, preparing a persuasive business plan is like playing a game. You must know and follow the official "rules"—the document form and format that make the most sense to the lender—and you must become skilled at anticipating and countering the other player's blocking moves. Additionally, before the game can even begin, you need to pass an ordeal: the executive summary of your business plan must make it past the initial screening.

Your executive summary must grab the reader's attention in just a few seconds. With just a glance, readers must be able to find the answers to their key questions and see that you're supplying data to back up the claims you're making.

Here are five tips to help you create an ultra-efficient, eye-catching summary:

1. **Stick to no more than a page.** That's the absolute maximum. If the business plan is already brief, you may be able to get away with half a page.

2. **State your main idea and your most compelling data up front.** Information in your summary doesn't need to appear in the same order as the information in your complete plan. Get straight to your boldest point and your juiciest evidence so your reader will want to keep reading.

3. **Use headings and bullets.** Design your summary for skimming, not reading. Keep your paragraphs short and break up content by inserting headings and using vertical lists.

4. **Highlight key points.** Strategically use bold type, text boxes, or underlining to call out critical information. Keep in mind that visual emphasis works only when it's applied sparingly. If you use bold type more than two or three times on a page, it loses its impact.

5. **Include numbers.** To entice your reader to check out your financial appendices, give them a taste of what they'll find there. Summarize your financial projections and the rationale behind them, providing a few key figures. A short chart may provide an efficient and eye-catching way to do this.

Sample One-page Business Plan

Lenders can differ widely in their preferred format for a business plan. A one-page plan like the one in Figure 9.5 could serve as a conversation starter in an early meeting, or it might serve as an attachment to an application form.

This short document could also provide an outline for a longer document; it includes most of the major headings one would expect to see in a more conventional plan.

Yip—The App for Dedicated Dog-Lovers	
Business Overview Yip is an iOS app that enables dog-lovers to spend as much time as possible with their pet. It locates dog-friendly spaces within a fixed radius and provides directions there. The app generates revenue through advertising, a premium subscription, and a Pet Passport game that collects fees from the dog-friendly sites a user visits.	**The Market** Young dog-owners (aged 20–35) form the largest and fastest-growing segment in a pet care market worth $70 billion. They like to take their pets wherever they go, including to stores, restaurants, and recreational facilities.
Competition While a few websites (such as DogsREverything) attempt to track dog-friendly spaces, their information is generally incomplete and not regularly updated, and their sites are not as easy to use as an app.	**Marketing Activities** • Blog • Social media (Facebook and Instagram) • Pop-up kiosks at pet stores • Paid advertising: pet store e-mail newsletters, Facebook, pet expos
Team • Ryan Pfeiffer, CEO • Justine Tremblay, Lead developer • Ava Singh, Director of Sales	**Expenses** • Computer hardware and software • Graphic design • Labor (specialized programmers) • Advertising • Travel to pet expos • Trademark
Two-year Action Plan • March 2020—Secure $150K in funding • September 2020—Launch beta product in Canada • December 2020—Launch final product in Canada • July 2020—Expand into the United States • September 2021—Sales of $50K • March 2022—Break-even	**Financials** • $50K already raised (government grant) • Incoming cash flow by December 2020 • Projections show break-even by March 2022 and profit by September 2022

Figure 9.5 One-page business plan

Checklist for a Business Plan

❑ Answers three key questions:
- ○ What is the opportunity?
- ○ Why is it significant?
- ○ How will the business pay the lender back?

❑ Presents the business case as an argument, based on claims and supporting evidence

❑ Logically connects evidence (data) to claims (main ideas)

❑ Provides detailed financials, historical and projected

❑ Spells out the meaning of financial data

❑ Provides all the information the lender needs to make a positive decision

❑ Anticipates and deflects possible objections
- ○ How do you know that's true?
- ○ Where did you get that data from?
- ○ So what?

❑ Emphasizes tangible impact

❑ Includes a concise executive summary

CHAPTER 10

White Papers

In a business context, as opposed to a government or research context, a white paper is a peculiar kind of report produced for marketing purposes. At first glance, it looks a lot like a standard technical report. A typical white paper:

- Addresses a complex technical topic
- Provides recommendations to solve a problem
- References research (conducted by the company and/or published by others)
- Runs to 5 to 20 pages
- Includes charts, tables, and/or diagrams

In form, a white paper resembles the kind of advisory document a technical consultant might produce for a client or an R&D engineer might create for the executive team. Its function, however, distinguishes it from such conventional recommendation reports. Whereas recommendation reports provide information to guide decision making, white papers assume the decision. Although they present themselves as scientific, objective documents, their intent is not merely to analyze or advise but to sell. *A white paper shows that a particular product or service provides the best possible solution to a particular problem so that readers want to engage with the company to find out more.*

An effective white paper performs a delicate balancing act, leveraging scientific authority for specific promotional purposes. Hazards present themselves on two fronts. If the white paper focuses too much on the science or technology, then it will fail to present the solution in a way that makes the audience realize and say, "Hey! That's just what I need to solve *my* problem!" The marketing opportunity is wasted. On the other hand, if a white paper sounds more like a flyer than a technical report, then it also loses its impact because it fails to gain the audience's trust.

In this chapter, you'll discover how to strike just the right balance a persuasive white paper requires. You'll learn how to use the white paper form to position your organization as an authority on a particular problem, provide scientific validation for your solution, and make your audience curious to learn more about that solution.

What Style of White Paper Will Best Suit Your Purpose?

Every white paper combines technical description with elements that serve a marketing purpose, but the proportion of these two components varies. Some white papers read like simplified versions of scientific articles, with only the length and the company logo distinguishing them as something different. Other white papers more closely resemble standard marketing collateral. These documents use a friendly, down-to-earth tone and vocabulary and present practical problem-solving information in terms accessible to a lay reader. They might include an action-oriented phrase such as "How to" or "Guide to" in their title.

In between these two extremes—the pseudo-article and the how-to guide—lies an entire spectrum of possible white paper styles. This chapter focuses on white papers created as marketing collateral, written to influence the customer or client who's in a position to make a buying decision. If you're writing for a different audience or with a different purpose, then you'll need to adapt some of the recommendations to suit your circumstances. Here are some examples of situations in which you might want to adopt a white paper style that leans more to the article side of the spectrum:

- You're seeking partners or employees with a research background, and you want your white paper to quickly bring them up to speed on your innovation.
- You're seeking funding from an investor with a research background, and you want to speak to them in a form that feels familiar to them.

- You're completing a patent application and are submitting the white paper as a way to document your innovation.
- You need an internal document that clearly explains your innovation so you can use that piece of writing as the base for creating external documents for raising funds and connecting with customers.

Note that this list doesn't include the desire to sound impressive or to establish yourself as the leading authority in the market. If your target audience is a potential buyer, then the best way to impress them and position yourself as the go-to authority in your field is to create a document that's easy to read and delivers valuable advice finely tuned to their situation.

Target a Specific Problem Your Audience Faces

A persuasive white paper holds up a mirror to your target audience. Looking into your description of a particular problem they face, they're able to recognize their dilemma and see how your solution could resolve their difficulties.

To help your reader identify with the problem and the solution you present, reverse-engineer the topic and structure of your white paper from the starting point of your audience's experience. Who are the people who can benefit the most from your product or services? How does your product or service help them?

Once you've done this groundwork, then you can work backward toward a description of your solution that highlights the most pertinent to your audience. For example, let's say your market comprises owners and managers of large apartment buildings who are frustrated by the amount of data entry and paper work required to manage maintenance requests from tenants. You offer the ideal solution: a smartphone app that tenants, property managers, and maintenance staff can use to monitor maintenance issues in real time. Figure 10.1 shows how you might work from your audience's perspective on the problem to reverse-engineer a product description that speaks to their specific needs.

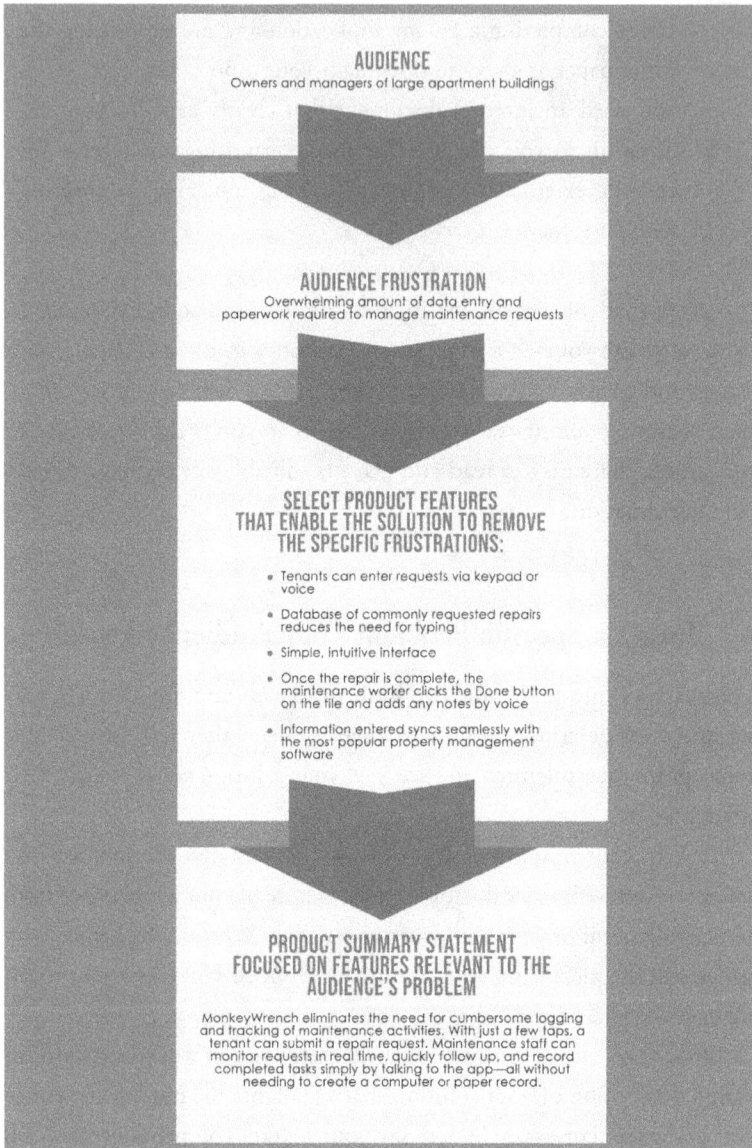

AUDIENCE
Owners and managers of large apartment buildings

AUDIENCE FRUSTRATION
Overwhelming amount of data entry and
paperwork required to manage maintenance requests

**SELECT PRODUCT FEATURES
THAT ENABLE THE SOLUTION TO REMOVE
THE SPECIFIC FRUSTRATIONS:**

- Tenants can enter requests via keypad or voice
- Database of commonly requested repairs reduces the need for typing
- Simple, intuitive interface
- Once the repair is complete, the maintenance worker clicks the Done button on the file and adds any notes by voice
- Information entered syncs seamlessly with the most popular property management software

**PRODUCT SUMMARY STATEMENT
FOCUSED ON FEATURES RELEVANT TO THE
AUDIENCE'S PROBLEM**

MonkeyWrench eliminates the need for cumbersome logging
and tracking of maintenance activities. With just a few taps, a
tenant can submit a repair request. Maintenance staff can
monitor requests in real time, quickly follow up, and record
completed tasks simply by talking to the app—all without
needing to create a computer or paper record.

Figure 10.1 Reverse-engineered structure for a white paper

The reverse-engineering process prevents you from making a common mistake that kills many white papers: the temptation to pack as many features as possible into the product description, whether or not they directly address the audience's concerns. Notice that the product summary statement in the example above zeroes in on just a few of MonkeyWrench's features and benefits. It doesn't mention some of the app's many other features—such as a customizable background and a built-in reminder tool—because those don't pertain to the particular problem the white paper focuses on, too much maintenance paper work.

Prioritize Usefulness

White paper authors often feel they must present the most comprehensive view of their product they can create, just in case a minor detail might pique the reader's interest. But persuasion requires precise aim, not a broad salvo. If you feel you need to pad out your product description "just in case," then ask yourself whether you're really ready to write a white paper. You probably need more insight into your audience before you're truly prepared to tell them how well your solution will serve them.

According to biotech entrepreneur Stephen Bartol, one of the benefits of writing a white paper is that it forces you to get up-close-and-personal with your audience's true needs. "It's a great way to learn what you don't know about your own industry," he says, "because you have to target a particular question or problem or issue."

Stephen should know. Between 2007 and 2017, he and his partner Chris Wybo ran Sentio, a company that grew out of Stephen's experience as an orthopedic surgeon. Together, this doctor and engineer duo developed a groundbreaking technology to locate nerves during surgery. They built a Detroit-based company that employed more than 18 engineers before it was acquired by Johnson and Johnson. (You can view a video of Sentio in use in the operating room here https://www.youtube.com/watch?v=EuOhREi9UkY&feature=youtu.be.)

During his 10 years with Sentio, Stephen was producing white papers "constantly." White papers served as key mechanisms for communicating with the lawyers who were filing patent applications on Sentio's behalf, with investors, and with customers. Because each of these audiences regarded the technology from a different angle, Stephen had to examine the needs of each group and tailor his white paper accordingly.

This meant a shift in perspective for someone who was used to forms of communication that mostly involved teaching and giving instructions. In order to connect with his target audiences, Stephen needed to fine-tune his listening skills. As a doctor, he was used to communicating with patients and colleagues from a position of recognized authority, thinking of communication mainly as "teaching" and "telling." But as a businessperson, he had to learn a different approach. Here's how he describes the mental shift he had to make:

> In medicine, we will listen to the patients to get our inputs, but then there's an internal process followed by communicating messages back to people, educating them, and teaching and telling them. In the business world, I found it's almost the opposite of that. It's a whole lot of listening. It's a whole lot of asking questions, learning from other people, and then taking that information and learning that comes from other people and trying to develop an answer that accommodates their needs. One that makes the best sense and is most helpful to them.

No matter how impressive you find your explanations and your visuals, in the end, your audience will read (and share) your white paper only if they find it useful. If you've developed avatars to guide your website writing, you may find those helpful aids as you create white papers. Learn, like Stephen, to listen to what your audience really needs and zero in on a significant problem they need help solving so your white paper can provide a sophisticated but accessible answer to that issue.

Give Advice in a Problem-to-solution Structure

Like a proposal, a white paper follows a problem-to-solution structure, with the problem described in such a way that it foreshadows the solution. But unlike a proposal, a white paper doesn't directly pitch the solution. Instead, it simply shows readers why the solution provides the optimal answer to their specific needs. In this way, it maintains the delicate balance between the alleged objectivity we expect of a scientific or technical document and the empathy that infuses persuasive writing with its power.

For instance, let's return to our example of the app to help apartment owners manage maintenance requests. If you're writing a proposal to pitch a property management company on the app, the outline for your document might look like this:

- Bernstein Property's maintenance concerns
- How MonkeyWrench can help

- Proposed configuration
- Costs
- Installation timeline
- Technical support
- Next steps

But if you're writing a white paper to interest various prospects in your technology, the above outline is too transaction-focused. Whereas a proposal aims to make a sale, a white paper sells the overall credibility and value of your solution. So an outline for a white paper describing the MonkeyWrench app might look something like this:

- The hidden costs of maintenance requests
- Possible solutions (Excel-based solution, desktop software, app)
- What to look for in a maintenance management app
- Cost savings with MonkeyWrench
- How to learn more

As a white paper author, your ultimate aim is to position yourself not as a salesperson but as a trusted partner or adviser. You do that not by asking for a purchase but by showing readers how deeply you understand their predicament and how well-equipped you are to advise them on a solution.

Be Savvy about How You Integrate References

As you present yourself as a trustworthy adviser, pay special attention to the way you cite and integrate information from other sources, such as studies you've conducted and research findings published by others. Those sources play a critical role in validating the claims you make about your solution. But bear in mind that simply adding a footnote will not invest your writing with the scientific authority a solid white paper conveys.

As always, the key is to tailor the way you present information to your audience. As you think about how best to integrate research sources into your writing, consider the scale of expertise that Anirudh Koul uses as he communicates with different audiences:

- **Novice**—Lay person with little or no technical knowledge related to a technology.

- **Ninja**—Skilled practitioners with deep technical knowledge in manipulating a technology. (Anirudh would consider himself a Ninja in the field of Artificial Intelligence.)
- **Guru**—Researcher engaged in creating new knowledge about the technology.

Before you insert your first quotation or footnote, ask yourself:

- Where are you along the spectrum from Novice to Guru?
- Where along the spectrum is your target audience?
- How broad is the gap between you?

The key to making the most of your research sources is integrating them into your white paper so they support your claims in a way that your target audience both understands and respects.

If you're a Guru who comes from a research background, here are a couple of pointers to keep in mind:

- Novices and Ninjas probably don't understand the shorthand of academic citation. Instead of simply citing sources by author name and date, briefly introduce each source and explain its relevance to your argument.
- Nonacademic readers will appreciate a simple citation style, not the style you're used to using for academic publications. A basic author-date system might suffice, or create your own style.

If you're a Ninja (skilled practitioner), here are a couple of tips for you:
- Don't try to write like a Guru if you aren't actually an academic expert. If there are any true Gurus in your audience, they'll immediately detect your fakery. It takes years of training to learn how to craft academic writing, which relies on certain conventions that are hard to replicate without the experience of preparing a doctoral dissertation.
- Embrace the perspective of an expert practitioner. Own your Ninja skills and experience by incorporating references to academic articles in a way that feels and sounds natural to you. Relate those references to your own observations and experience.

- Choose your references carefully. Because a nonresearcher can't easily distinguish a poorly designed study from a well-designed study, look for corroboration of the sources you integrate into writing.

And what if you're neither a Ninja nor a Guru but someone at the Novice end of the scale? Then I'm sorry, but you're not really qualified to write the white paper you have in mind. You might consider partnering with someone who has the required level of experience so you can authentically present your product or service as a research-backed solution.

Speak Your Audience's Language

Now that he's exited Sentio, Stephen passes his white paper experience on to other innovative entrepreneurs whom he mentors. He gives his mentees this fundamental piece of advice: "Get over yourself and stop writing so much. No one wants to read endless descriptions of things. Try to keep things as simple as possible."

Easier said than done when you're dealing with a complex product or service. But here's the irony all white paper writers face: the more complex your solution, the more simply and clearly you must present it. To tackle that conundrum, start by figuring out what Stephen calls the audience's "level of sophistication" with regard to your solution and then tweak your style choices to match that.

Your writing style should mirror as closely as possible the style your readers are most familiar with so that you come across as someone who understands their problem from an insider's perspective. Show you are fluent in their professional language. For instance, in a white paper describing Sentio to chief surgeons, you might incorporate academic sources as well as jargon from the OR. In contrast, in a white paper explaining the same technology to an investment firm, you'd want to downplay medical lingo and use business terms, such as "speed to market" and "ROI" (return on investment).

A great way to communicate complex concepts clearly and economically is to use visual language. Think beyond data-driven diagrams, such as charts and tables, and consider how you can visually represent frameworks, models, process flows, and relationships. For instance, rather than describing a five-step data entry process, why not illustrate that process through a simple infographic? Instead of trying to "talk" your readers through the tiered components of a software system, how about showing its elements as nested circles?

If communicating through such visual language doesn't come easily to you, challenge yourself to build up skills in this area. A good place to start is *Infographics: The Power of Visual Storytelling* by Jason Lankow, Josh Ritchie, and Ross Crooks.

Aim to Start a Conversation

Like a pitch or a proposal, a white paper should end by inspiring a beginning. It should leave the reader wanting to learn more about the expertise and the particular solution you have to offer.

When raising money for Sentio, Stephen often used a white paper as an intentional stepping stone to a focused meeting with an investor. When giving a live pitch, he'd provide the white paper as a handout. The goal of the pitch was to interest the audience in reading the white paper, and the goal of the white paper was then to secure an in-depth conversation with the investor.

As you produce your white papers, keep the big picture of your marketing and sales process top-of-mind. How will the document fit into the chain of interactions that leads a prospect from initial curiosity about your company to a sales conversation with you?

And remember to let your audience know how they can start a conversation with you. Include a clear call to action at the bottom of your final page so that the readers you've worked so hard to entice will know what to do next to connect with you and learn more about the solution you've described so compellingly to them.

Contrasting White Paper Styles

Figure 10.2 shows an excerpt from the draft of a government white paper, contrasted with a revision targeting a business audience. Notice how the different styles affect choices in content, tone, vocabulary, visual design.

Here are some questions to reflect on as you read the two examples:

- Which style do you prefer?
- Which style would feel most familiar and easy to your target audience?
- How closely does your style preference align with your audience's preference? If there's a gap between them, how do you need to adapt to connect more effectively with your audience?

Version 1: Excerpt from *Improving Cybersecurity of Managed Service Providers: Supporting Small- and Medium-Size Businesses*[1]

The MSP market has seen tremendous growth over the past 6 years. This success has resulted in MSPs increasingly becoming targets of cybersecurity attacks that can impact their business and their customers' overall trust in MSPs and jeopardize their customers' security. For example, a recent attack on MSPs, commonly referred to as Cloud Hopper, may have exposed the information that MSPs held describing their customers' IT infrastructures and account information.

The research conducted for this project indicates that a typical MSP focuses primarily on ensuring that it can provide the best options for remotely managing SMBs' IT and end-user systems and that cybersecurity of their own IT infrastructure may be a secondary concern. The research was informed discussions with subject matter experts (SMEs) in the MSP market and included interviews, correspondence with MSPs, summaries from MSP-focused conferences, and vendors for back-office and customer technical support such as remote monitoring and management, professional service automation, and automated backup tools. The research led the NCCoE SMEs to identify the list of Cybersecurity Framework Subcategories listed in the Scope section of this document.

For example, after discussions with SMEs within the MSP market, the NCCoE's technical experts concluded that many MSP IT infrastructures are implemented on nonsegmented networks. These networks are generally undesirable because they enable equal network access to all assets on the network. If the network were compromised, nonsegmented networking enables the spread of malware by creating a corporate-wide horizontal network. Nonsegmented networking also allows user access to all corporate assets by default, which greatly increases the potential for unwanted user activity. Figure 10.3 depicts an example of a nonsegmented network to illustrate this research finding…

---

[1]K. Waltermire and H. Perper. October, 2019. *Improving Cybersecurity of Managed Service Providers: Supporting Small- and Medium-Size Businesses* (draft) (National Cybersecurity Center of Excellence.   https://www.nccoe.nist.gov/sites/default/files/library/project-descriptions/msp-ic-project-description-draft.pdf, (accessed October 12, 2019).

Figure 10.2 Two versions of a white paper

Version 2: Revision targeting a business audience (leaders of MSPs)

> *Shortened sentences and paragraphs improve readability.*

As the MSP market has grown over the past 6 years, so have the number of cybersecurity attacks. The recent Cloud Hopper hack was just one instance. Such attacks are becoming more common, and they jeopardize more than just customer IT infrastructures and account information. They undermine customers' overall trust in MSPs.

> *Clear statement of the problem the audience faces.*

> *I'm a fan of contractions because they create a relaxed, conversational tone that sounds like natural speech.*

A Threat That's Easily Overlooked

> *Headings make the document easy to skim and also draw attention to key ideas.*

> *It's important to express the problem with empathy.*

The day-to-day demands of remotely managing a SME's IT and end-user system typically take up most of a CIO's time. These days, it's not enough to keep up with your customer's needs; you want to stay one step ahead so you can offer them the best options and help their business thrive.

> *The tone stays nonjudgemental here. The problem—overlooking the risk of nonsegmented networks—has arisen for good reason. Ignoring that could potentially make the reader feel as if the white paper is blaming them.*

We collected information from more than 120 MSPs across the United States and 30 vendors of back-office and customer technical support. More than 75 percent of them admitted that cybersecurity ranked "medium-priority" or "low-priority" on their weekly agenda.

> *Notice the way the research is framed and summarized here. A government audience of researchers will be interested in the methodology behind the study, but a business audience will want to know the highlights.*

Nonsegmented Networks Pose a Particular Risk

> *It's a good practice to introduce a diagram by stating what you mean it to show. Don't leave it up to the reader to guess at how to interpret a chart or visual.*

Many MSP's IT infrastructures rely on nonsegmented networks. While these have the advantage of allowing equal access to all assets on the network, with that convenience comes more risk. When a nonsegmented network becomes compromised, malware can quickly spread through a corporate-wide horizontal network. Nonsegmented networking also allows default user access to all corporate assets, creating great potential for unwanted user activity.

> *The language in the business version is more direct than in the government version.*

Figure 1 illustrates how a nonsegmented network puts an MSP at risk.

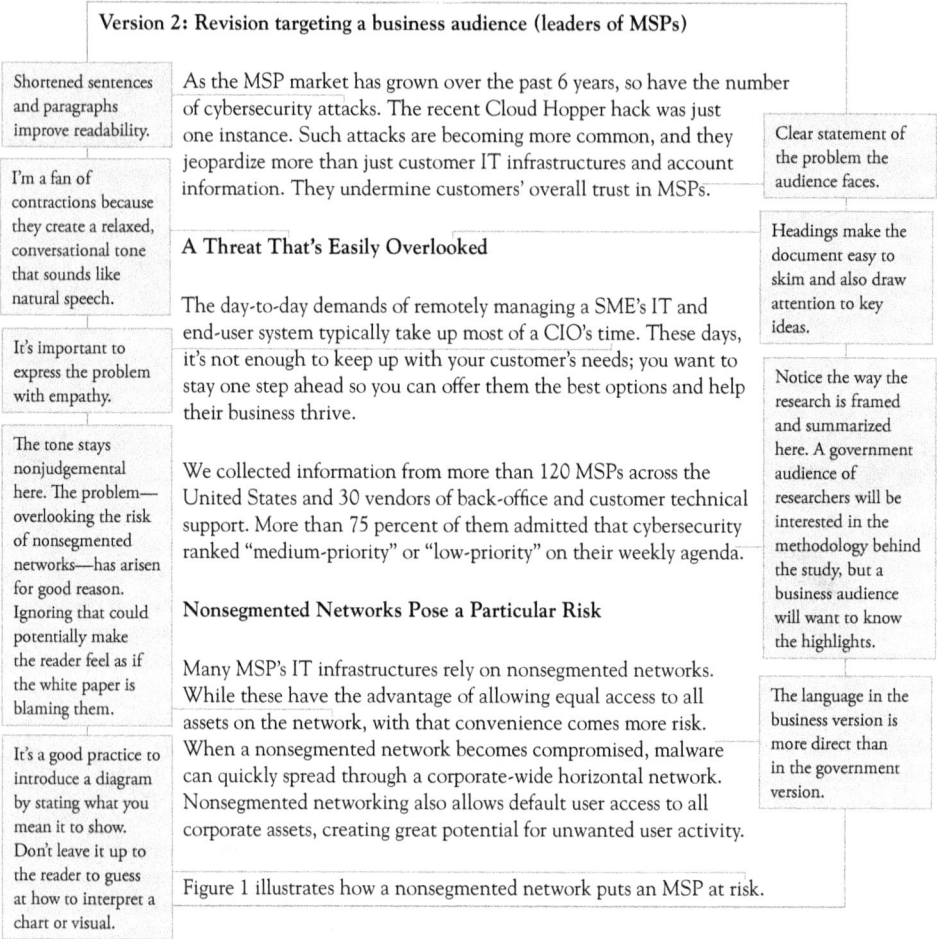

Figure 10.2 (Continued)

Checklist for White Papers

❏ Matches the style of white paper to the audience and purpose
❏ Targets a specific audience and problem they're facing
❏ Describes the ideal solution to the problem
❏ Includes only information that's useful to the audience
❏ Positions the writer as an authority on solving the problem
❏ Follows a problem-to-solution structure
❏ Presents helpful background information and advice, not a sales pitch
❏ Backs up claims with research-based evidence
❏ Integrates references in a way that makes them intelligible and earns the audience's respect
❏ Speaks the audience's language
❏ Communicates key points through visuals (charts, tables, and/or diagrams)
❏ Includes a call to action

CHAPTER 11

One-Pagers

Every marketing toolkit needs a one-pager, or a "one-sheet" as this sophis-ticated version of a flyer is sometimes called. Like a flyer, a one-pager is a promotional tool that uses a catchy headline and graphics to grab the audience's attention. But while a flyer typically announces a single event or promotion, a one-pager promotes either your company, or a particular product or service, as a whole.

A well-designed one-pager can serve many different situations. For example, you might e-mail an electronic version to a prospect after an initial conversation. If you participate in trade shows or exhibitions, you'll want a printed stack of one-pagers for your table. And if you're looking for a way to create a focal point for a meeting with a potential customer, a one-pager can help with that as well.

One-pagers come in a few different formats, suitable for different audiences and purposes. If you're pitching an investor, you may want to create one-page summary of your pitch to either precede or supplement your pitch deck. If you sell services to large corporations, then you may be asked for a one-page "capability statement," which provides a resume-like description of your company's core competencies. Some one-pagers are actually two-pagers; they use the front of the sheet to grab the audience's attention and the reverse to feature details and customer testimonials.

In this chapter, we'll focus on one particular kind of one-pager, the promotional one-sheet that describes a particular service, product, or event. See Figure 11.1 for an example.

As you can see, if you want to create something visually appealing, a single page doesn't allow room for much text. Producing a one-pager will challenge your ability to communicate your key messages clearly and

Figure 11.1 Sample one-pager

concisely. You must make each syllable count because a crowded layout makes you seem disorganized, unfocused, and inconsiderate. It signals readers that you don't care enough to give them a document that's attractive and easy to read.

Because the visual aspect of one-pagers matters so much, we'll start there, with some basic guidelines you can use to create a professional-quality document, even if you can't afford a professional designer. You'll also learn how to craft a laser-focused message, adopt a minimalist writing style, and incorporate persuasive testimonials.

Before we begin, you might be wondering, "Do I need a professional designer to create a one-pager?" In the perfect world, yes, you'd have the budget to engage a professional designer. However, with the drag-and-drop design tools now available online, it's also possible to produce a professional-quality one-pager on your own, using a free or low-cost template as your base. If you haven't yet checked out low-cost online tools such as Canva and PicMonkey, I'd encourage you to give one or both of those free programs a try. You may be surprised to discover how easy it is to create branded, eye-catching documents to market your business.

Basic Design Guidelines

Humans are emotional beings, and we react to the world around us and the objects in it, emotionally. As cognitive scientist Donald Norman has shown, when you design a product to engage users emotionally, you don't just attract more people to your product. What Norman calls "emotional design" also results in items that produce better outcomes because they're easier and more pleasurable to use.[1]

Make the logic of emotional design work for you as you draft your one-pagers. Pull out all the visual design stops to entice your audience and create a reading experience that's aesthetically enjoyable. By spending time and effort on visual design, you'll produce one-pagers that not only look better than nondescript documents but also communicate better.

Below are a few basic design principles you can use to produce attractive one-pagers. I've grouped them into four key categories: page layout, colors, shapes, and fonts.

1. **Page layout.** Allow a generous amount of empty space (whitespace) as padding around your text and visuals. The surest way to turn readers

[1]D. Norman. 2004. "Attractive Things Work Better," in *Emotional Design: Why We Love (or Hate) Everyday Things* (New York, NY: Basic Books), pp. 17–33.

off is to cram too much content onto your single page. If readers have to squint to find out what you have to say, they won't bother.

The best way to make sure you allow enough whitespace is to *commit to your margins*. Set a generous border around your page—at least an inch all the way around—and don't fiddle with it, no matter how tempting it is to try to squeeze just one more line of text in. Instead of adding words, trim your copy. (See below for pointers on creating a minimalist writing style.)

As you arrange your content on the page, aim for balance rather than perfect symmetry. Some of the most pleasing designs are slightly asymmetrical. That's why professional designers typically view a page "grid" in terms of thirds rather than quarters.

2. **Colors.** This may sound obvious, but I'll say it anyway because I see so many one-pagers that violate this fundamental principle: use the same color palette for your one-pager that you use for your website and other marketing materials.

What if you designed your website a while back, and you're no longer in love with its color scheme? Or you want the product your one-pager promotes to have its own visual brand? In both these cases, you can use your brand's main color palette as a base and freshen it up with one or two new colors. That way, you can create something new while maintaining ties to the old, creating a visual consistency that helps build trust as well as brand recognition.

Limit the total number of colors in your palette to no more than five. Go beyond that and you'll create visual chaos.

3. **Shapes.** The simplest way to lay out a one-pager is to work with squares and rectangles. They're easy to balance and maneuver on the page. However, they also create a hard-edged, boxed-in aesthetic.

That kind of "look and feel" might work just fine for your brand and your audience, especially if you're designing for a corporate audience. But if you want to convey more playfulness or creativity, then you'll want to experiment with other shapes as well. Circles work well for brands associated with holistic, integrated approaches or organic processes. Triangles convey a sense of sharp focus. And infographic-style visuals enable you to combine multiple shapes into an eye-catching image.

How and where should you use shapes in a one-pager? Shapes can show up effectively as background images, as backgrounds to text boxes, in headers or footers, and in key diagrams. As you group your content into sections for your document, consider the different shape each grouping could take. For instance, if you want to compare two versions of your product, you could group that content into a table, two square text boxes side by side, two text boxes with rounded edges, two circles overlapping at the edges, two columns of text, and so on and so on.

4. **Fonts.** Repeat after me: No shrinking the font size to squeeze in more content! Along with ample white space, legible fonts play a vital role in making your one-pager easy (and therefore enjoyable) to read.

Use a minimum font size of 12 points, larger if you think your one-pager will mainly circulate electronically. Many web designers use 14-point font as their standard, so that can serve as a useful benchmark.

Besides size, you face two other font choices: the number of fonts you'll include in your one-pager and the font style or styles you'll use.

If you'd like to differentiate headings from paragraphs, then you could use a different heading for each kind of text. But make two fonts your max—more than that will, like too many colors, create a sense of disorganization and confusion. It's also perfectly ok to stick with a single font throughout your document. That can create an impression of unity that might be important to your brand.

As for font style, just as your one-pager color palette should conform to the branding you use elsewhere, so should your font selection. Without access to professional design software and font packages, you may not be able to perfectly match your one-pager font to your website font, but you should be able to come close.

Improve the Quality of Your Designs
Through "Multitracking"

The design process is meant to be messy. Trying to force it into neatness can hamper creativity and compromise the final result. It's particularly important not to narrow your options too quickly. In fact, research has found that iterating on two or three designs at once will give you the best output in the long run.

Chris and Chip Heath, authors of *Decisive: How to Make Better Choices in Life and Work*, call this approach "multitracking."[1] Although it may feel like time-wasting to work on multiple designs simultaneously, a 2010 study of graphic designers creating Web banner ads proved the opposite.[2]

The study pitted two teams of designers against each other (33 participants in total). The first team followed a "serial" process; they created one banner and then revised it five times. The second team also created six versions of the banner but worked using a "parallel" process; they created three banners, revised two of them, and then chose one of those two to revise again. When the ads ran on MySpace.com, those created via the parallel approach outperformed the other ads in terms of click-through rates and time spent on the target site (the site to which the ad directed users). They also received higher ratings from advertising professionals.

Multitracking also yielded additional benefits for the novice designers who participated in the study: it correlated with an increase in their "self-efficacy," their confidence in their design abilities. On the other hand, those who followed the serial approach experienced a decrease in their self-efficacy. In other words, intentionally exploring multiple design options won't just result in a better product but will also make you a more confident designer able to learn from feedback and continually develop your skills.

---

[1] C. Heath and D. Heath. 2013. *Decisive: How to Make Better Choices in Life and Work* (Toronto, Canada: Random House), Chapter 3, Kindle.

[2] S. Dow, A. Glassco, J. Kass, M. Schwarz, D.L. Schwarz, S.R. Klemmer. 2010. "Parallel Prototyping Leads to Better Design Results, More Divergence, and Increased Self-Efficacy," *ACM Transactions on Computer-Human Interaction* 17, no. 4, pp. 18:1–24.

Four Tips for Laser-Focused Messaging

You've created a spacious layout, with generous margins around the sheet edges, the paragraphs, and graphic elements. You've also chosen a legible font, at least 12 points in size. The placeholder images and text look great, but how on earth are you going to fit everything you want to say into the small amount of space you have available for copy?

Here's the brutal answer: you're not. You're going to have to adjust your notion of "everything you want to say" to fit the constraints of your design. That may sound daunting, but if you work with the restrictions instead of against them, you'll develop laser-focused messaging that will cut right to the core of what matters most to your target audience.

To make the most of every square inch of your one-pager, follow these four tips:

1. **Focus on the next step, not the sale.** In most situations, a one-pager doesn't aim to produce an instant sale. It simply guides the audience one step further along the sales process. All your messaging needs to do, then, is persuade readers to take the desired next step.

    For instance, a prospect might pick up your one-pager at a trade show and read it to learn about your product for the first time. Or a potential client might receive your one-sheet following an exploratory conversation. In both of these cases, the one-pager just needs to intrigue the audience so you can engage them in a more in-depth conversation, which could potentially evolve into a sales conversation.

    Focusing on one step in the customer journey, instead of the final destination, means your content doesn't need to cover all the ins and outs of what you're offering. It just needs to rouse a teeny bit of interest and desire, just enough to motivate the reader to move one step closer to buying.

2. **Include a clear call to action (CTA).** Your call to action clearly directs your audience toward that next small step you want them to take. Your CTA shouldn't appear like a neon flashing sign overwhelming your key message. You don't need a giant typeface or a fancy graphic to steer readers in the right direction. Simply tell

readers what to do next, in a friendly, conversational tone. Here are some examples of CTAs that could work well at the bottom of a one-pager:

- For a customized quote, give us a call at...
- For more information about our custom packages, visit our website at ...
- Curious about how we could help you? E-mail us for a free consult...
- To learn more, visit [URL]...
- Ready to get serious about [solving a problem]? Check out our starter program at [URL]...

3. **Choose a headline that evokes emotion.** Think of a one-pager as a one-glance document. You get just seconds (maybe split-seconds) to make a positive visual impression and lure your audience into reading your copy. A headline that's too long (more than about 10 words) will make your design seem crowded and unappealing. And one that lacks emotional "oomph" will also fail to attract attention.

To infuse your headline with emotion, start by identifying the emotional reaction you want it to produce. Strong headlines often evoke fear, curiosity, or desire. Consider the examples in Figure 11.2:

Fear	• Are your bottling machines missing this critical safety device? • Stop your next cyber security crisis before it starts • How many profit leaks are stealing your revenues?
Curiosity	• The new marketing tool your competitors hope you never discover • Create motivating compliance training that really works • No more half-video calls!
Desire	• Uncover the hidden sales waiting in your pipeline • Reduce your carbon tax by 15% this year • Turn your house into a Smart Home with just one click

Figure 11.2 Headlines that stir up emotion

For more tips on creating power headlines, revisit the tips in Chapter 3.

4. **Use the Think/Feel/Do Test.** You can use this test with any business document, but it works especially well for documents with a narrow, instrumental focus, such as one-pagers. With your eye fixed on the

outcome you want to result from your one-pager, ask yourself how you want readers to react immediately after reading your document:

- What should your readers be thinking?
- How should they be feeling?
- What should they be doing?

If you've crafted a laser-sharp message and a unified design, then you should be able to answer each of these questions with a few specific words or phrases. For instance, let's say you've just created a one-pager on cloud-based software to help independent graphic designers manage their digital assets. Right after your audience reads your one-pager:

- They should be thinking: "I absolutely need this time-saving tool!"
- They should be feeling: "What a relief to know there's an easy, affordable way for me to get organized!"
- They should be doing the step outlined in your CTA: "I'm going to check out the website so I can get more details!"

Remember, your one-pager aims to persuade your audience to take one small step. If you find yourself producing long, rambling responses to the Think/Feel/Do questions, then your one-pager hasn't passed the test. You're probably trying to achieve too much at once; you may need to go back to the drafting board to clarify your purpose and refocus your design and message.

Be Prepared to Iterate and Collaborate

Valerie Song is CEO of AVA Technologies, a Vancouver startup that has raised more than $2 million to develop and launch smart indoor gardening products. (You can check out their emerging product line of self-lighting and self-irrigating gardening containers at https://www.avagrows.com/.) Because AVA targets consumers who are seeking a sophisticated aesthetic in home décor, Valerie and her team have prioritized from the beginning the visual design of their website, packaging, and print collateral. Their startup team includes an in-house graphic designer, Kelsey Snowdon.

When AVA designs print collateral for a new product, they follow a five-phase, iterative process that involves Kelsey and other team members as well as multiple rounds of input from the target audience.

1. **Phase 1: Goal-setting.** Valerie and her team set one key, measurable business goal, which becomes a success indicator. Here's how Valerie explains this fundamental stage:

   > At the end of the day, a great design for a business means that you've accomplished the goals you set out at the beginning of the design process. The number one thing for me is "What is your goal that you're trying to communicate or the action you're trying to get the other person to do?" If your package is going to be on the shelf, you want the person to buy your product. If your sell sheet is going to be at a trade show, you're trying to get the retailer to pick up your products.

2. **Phase 2: Customer research.** Kelsey learns all she can about AVA's customers and their values with regards to the product the one-pager describes. According to Valerie, it takes time and effort to do this crucial stage right:

   > Always stand in the shoes of your audience, or, better yet, find people who are in those positions—a friend or someone from your extended network—and ask them what they think. It's always an iterative process.

3. **Phase 3: Strategy and prototyping.** Drawing on the customer research, Kelsey develops a design strategy that will appeal to the target audience. This strategy enables her to create sketches and mock-ups so everyone involved in the design process can agree on the direction the design will take.

4. **Phase 4: Graphic design.** Once the design direction has been developed and the expectations set, Kelsey is ready to start building out the final design.

5. **Phase 5: Testing and feedback.** AVA executes the design and then collects information on how customers respond to it. Through testing different versions of the design (conducting A/B testing), they adjust the content and layout as necessary. The key, says Valerie, is to look for patterns that point to key information people are seeking: "Make sure you address all the key questions, and then test, talk to people, iterate, and then finalize."

Feedback patterns may point to issues with "information hierarchy." If people are missing your key points, Kelsey notes, that may be because of the way you've visually grouped your information, applied color, or used different type sizes. Misplaced visual emphasis can cause people to miss the message you're trying to get across, even if your wording is clear.

Customer feedback may also point up other ways the visual design fails to connect with the intended audience. For example, if you choose a stock photo featuring a model who doesn't represent your target demographic, you could alienate customers without realizing it. As Kelsey says, "People want to see themselves and their dream lives reflected in your marketing—not a life they can't recognize."

For a simple design project, the process outlined above could start with a design brief from Valerie, a document describing the business goal and criteria that will spell success. Or for more complex projects, Kelsey might work with the team on a cross-functional design sprint. Either way, Valerie stresses that close collaboration is a must:

It's not enough to just hand over a piece of paper to a designer and expect them to do the design. There's the upfront meeting to communicate your objectives, and there are checkpoints every step of the way, or you're going to end up with someone that spent a lot of time delivering something that you didn't want. Thorough upfront research, setting clear objectives, and creating a good brand strategy should translate to great business results.

How to Write in a Minimalist Style

If you haven't yet read Chapter 4, on writing for the web, this would be a great time to check it out. The same "letting go of the words" approach that applies to producing web copy will also help you create the minimalist style one-pagers require.

Here are five reminders I give myself whenever I'm working on a one-pager:

1. **If there's a shorter word, use it.** Plain, ordinary words (like *get* and *buy*) trump fancier words (like *obtain* and *purchase*.).

2. **If you can cut a word, cut it.** Be ruthless. Watch particularly for three culprits that create wordiness:

   - **"There is/are..."** Avoid this throat-clearing phrase and just say what you have to say. "There are three reasons that explain these results" easily becomes "Three reasons explain these results."

   - **"That."** Sometimes, you do need this handy relative pronoun for clarity's sake. But many sentences sound perfectly clear without it. "We can provide the help that you need" is five characters longer but no clearer than "We can provide the help you need."

   - **Low-value adjectives and adverbs.** When we're writing to sell, it's natural to load up our sentences with words that add color. We want to intensify meaning, and adding an adjective or adverb seems a simple way to do that. But many of these modifiers (describing words) add little real value to the copy.

     Be alert for modifier pile-ups, like this: "Our team wants you to have a wildly [adverb] profitable [adjective] and successful [adjective] year." A leaner alternative prunes away the describing words, creating a more direct and conversational style: *We want to help make this your most profitable year yet.* Also beware of modifiers that don't really add any value at all because their meaning is imprecise. Examples include *very, quite, significantly, dramatically, phenomenally*, and *greatly.* Rather than padding your sentences with such empty-syllable words, try to quantify your meaning instead. For instance, if your product will "greatly improve" soil pH, give us some numbers to describe what "significant" really means.

3. **If you can turn a paragraph into a list, do it.** While you want to be careful not to turn your one-pager into a listicle (an article that's one long list), you want to keep paragraphs as short as you can. That means turning at least some of your content into bulleted points. Make sure, though, that the content you present as a list deserves

emphasis because the whitespace surrounding list items will attract the reader's eye.

4. **Conversational and concise is sometimes better than correct.** Did you notice the usage error in point #1 above? Technically, the phrase "Plain ordinary words, like 'get' and 'buy'" should read "Plain, ordinary words, such as 'get' and 'buy'." In correct English, "like" should introduce a comparison, not an example. However, I chose to break a so-called "rule" because most of us swap "like" for "such as" when we're speaking informally.[2]

5. **Ask for help from a second reader.** Once you've trimmed your writing as closely as you can, ask someone else to review it. Almost certainly, a fresh set of eyes will find some additional words or syllables to pare away.

The Importance of Testimonials

As we've seen, a one-pager doesn't allow you enough space to dive deeply into any one aspect of your product or service. Nor does it give you room to support your claims about your offerings with hard data. This is *not* the ideal opportunity to show off graphs and tables illustrating the technical effectiveness of what you're selling. Save those for more detailed sales documents, white papers, and presentations.

To intrigue your audience and convince them to engage with you further, you do need to offer them some kind of "proof" that your product or service delivers on your promises. But that "proof" needs to make emotional not logical sense.

Client or customer testimonials fit that bill. They validate the claims you make about your offerings in a way that tugs on a three powerful persuasion levers:

- **They invoke the power of story**. As Jonathan Gottschall demonstrates in *The Storytelling Animal*, "We are, as a species, addicted

---

[2]Joseph Williams explores and deflates the social construction of grammatical "errors" in his often-cited essay, "The Phenomenology of Error," *College Composition and Communication* 32, no. 2 (May 1981), pp.152–168.

to story." Testimonials exploit the universal attraction to narrative by capturing, in just a couple of sentences, customer success stories. Those instantly grab readers' attention because our brains are hard-wired to notice stories and to remember them.[3]

- **They encourage identification**. We tend to trust (and buy from) people who remind us of ourselves. By including testimonials from prospects who closely resemble your target audience, you encourage potential customers to feel a kind of kinship with you and your organization.

- **They supply "social proof."** According to social proof theory, when we don't know what to do, we look around us to see what others are doing and base our decision on their behavior.[4] Testimonials like the one in Figure 11.3 show potential customers they can trust a decision to work with you because others have made that decision before them, and it paid off.

To get the most bang from your testimonial buck, document your testimonials and make them precise. For each customer story, include the customer's complete name, job title, and/or organization. (Testimonials without such legitimating information aren't really worth much.) Mention specific benefits the customer achieved so readers can perceive, the tangible value your products or services deliver. ("We increased our profits by 23% in the first year" beats "It was a great experience all-round!")

You may find you need to coach your testimonial-givers or edit (with their permission) the words they initially provide. Most people who are willing to give a testimonial are also willing to work with you to make it impactful. In fact, many people appreciate having some guidelines to work within. When you ask for a testimonial, consider the kind of proof you'd like it to offer and share that purpose. This is especially important if

---

[3]J. Gottschall. 2013. *The Storytelling Animal: How Stories Make Us Human* (New York, NY: Houghton Mifflin/Mariner Books), Preface, Kindle.

[4]Psychologist Robert Cialdini gives an in-depth description of how social proof works in *Influence: The Psychology of Persuasion* (New York, NY: William Morrow, 1993), pp. 114–166.

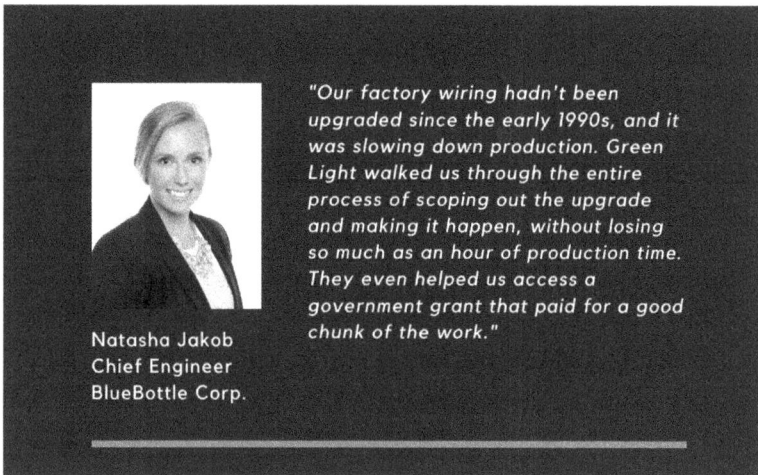

Figure 11.3 Sample testimonial from a one-pager

you provide a number of products or services and your one-pager focuses on just one of these. For instance, let's say you deliver both consulting services and a line of products. If your one-pager focuses on your product line, then make sure your testimonials show the benefits that come from using a specific product, not from accessing the personal expertise and advice of a consultant.

The Many Returns of a One-Pager

Because effective one-pagers pack so much influence into such a small space, you'll learn a lot from creating them. Producing an emotionally engaging one-pager gives you practice applying techniques of graphic design, honing your key messages, and streamlining your writing style. The upfront investment may seem costly, especially if you're hiring a graphic designer, but the ROI includes skills that will make you a stronger writer across the whole gamut of persuasive writing you produce to drive your business forward.

And as your business moves ahead, your one-pager will serve as a living document that enables you to continually test and refine your messaging and your products. Your one-pager, like your other marketing collateral, should evolve as you learn more about your market and your business responds to what you learn.

Checklist for One-Pagers

❑ Spacious page layout, with margins of at least an inch all around the document

❑ Font size of at least 10-point throughout

❑ Balanced (though not necessarily symmetrical) distribution of text and visuals

❑ Color palette aligned with company branding

❑ No more than five colors in the document

❑ Clear goal and call to action

❑ Headline that evokes emotion

❑ Minimalist, conversational writing style

❑ Testimonial(s)

Use the Think/Feel/Do test:

- What should your readers be thinking?
- How should they be feeling?
- What should they be doing?

CHAPTER 12

Training Material

When I think back on my first year as a university professor, I feel like sending an apology note to each student I taught. Or, rather, failed to teach. When I entered the classroom fresh from my dissertation research, I had deep insight into the inner workings of literature and culture but zero understanding of how to communicate those insights to other people. Especially undergraduates who had little interest in the fiction, poetry, and drama on the syllabus for English 101.

To make matters worse, as someone who'd always been a super-keen student, I couldn't relate to my students' lack of enthusiasm for the course of study I'd laid out. How could it be possible for someone to read Shakespeare or Faulkner and remain unmoved? Or to not even bother to read them in the first place?

As I started to recognize the breadth of the divide that separated me from my students, I became frustrated and discouraged. Classes started to feel like either pleas or stand-offs, with me trying desperately to attract student attention while defending the value of the course content. I felt like I was trying to communicate with aliens—and I'm guessing that my students probably thought I was also an alien speaking in a language completely foreign and irrelevant to them.

What a missed opportunity for all of us. With 20 years of teaching hindsight, I now realize that the gap between my students and me wasn't the problem. That gap exists in all teaching situations because the goal of instruction is to create a bridge from ignorance to knowledge, from the territory of the novice to the territory of the expert. The real problem was my inability to view the course content through the eyes of the students and meet the learners where they were, not where I thought they should have been.

As a rookie professor, I didn't know then what I understand now about how the brain works. Neurologically, the only way we can learn something new is to connect with something we already know, to build on or modify the existing neuronal networks that have formed through prior learning.[1] When we're teaching, our number-one job is to figure out how to make that link happen. That's the secret to engaging learners, helping them remember what we're teaching, and motivating them to apply what they're learning to their personal circumstances.

In this chapter, I'll share with you five core principles you can use as you develop training materials to support your products and services. Those materials might include live workshops, instruction manuals, online courses, or video tutorials. Whatever form your "training" takes, the core principles will enable you to produce content that connects with your audience and turns them into raving fans of whatever product or service you're teaching them about.

Principle 1: Meet Your Audience Where They Are

When you started your business, you probably had an ideal customer in mind. But how many of your current customers perfectly match that profile? As you've interacted with your market, you've probably had to adjust your preconceptions and adapt to the specific needs of the real customers in front of you.

When you design training materials, you may also start with an ideal learner, someone who's interested in developing the knowledge and skills you have to teach and brings a certain level of knowledge and experience to the table. But it's wise to check that profile against reality. Here are a few harsh truths you'll need to face if you want to develop training materials that engage and help real readers:

- **Most learners are rushed.** Even learners who are interested in your topic probably don't have the time they wish they had to explore it.

---

[1]For a concise overview of the role of neuronal networks in learning, see R.J. Wlodkowski. *Enhancing Adult Motivation to Learn*, 3rd ed. (San Francisco, CA: Jossey-Bass), pp. 8–13.

Your readers want to be able to access key information quickly so they can quickly master the concepts and skills they need.

- **Few people care about "theory" and "background."** As someone who's created a complex product or service, you probably care deeply about its origins in theoretical principles or underlying technology. But people reading your training materials don't want complex explanations; they're looking for straightforward content that will help them perform real-world tasks. Save your background "theory" for conference presentations or white papers, and keep your focus on the practical.

- **Learners don't always show up with the knowledge you'd expect.** I once taught a business writing course in Nigeria that was designed for people with advanced English proficiency and a university education. The real learners who showed up included professionals with master's degrees from British and American universities as well as nomadic herdsmen whose formal education probably ended with elementary school. Although the diversity in that group may seem extreme, I've encountered an equally wide span of knowledge and experience in almost every group I've taught. Recognize that your training materials may need to teach people who lack some of the basics you might assume as a given.

- **People need help "connecting the dots."** When I consult with clients as a learning designer, my chief task is to translate the knowledge of "subject matter experts," or SMEs (pronounced *smees*), into content that novices can easily access and use. To do this, I ask a lot of questions, to the point that SMEs sometimes get a bit frustrated with me. Once they've shared their high-level perspective on the given topic, they tend to have little patience for walking through the details of how to pull practical insights from that knowledge and apply it in particular circumstances.

  As the SME on your own products or services, you may share that impatience. But get over it. When you're creating training materials, you can't expect learners, who lack your expertise and experience, to intuitively make the leap from high-level concepts to hands-on practice. They need you to connect the dots for them through step-by-step instruction, examples, and practice opportunities.

- **Many of us are scared to try new things.** Despite everything positive psychology has taught us, I am frequently amazed by how many people underestimate the importance of cultivating a positive mindset among learners. True, some of us love learning for learning's sake, but for most people, learning can be a daunting, even painful experience. Mastering new concepts and skills tends to mean hard work, and many of us feel clumsy and embarrassed as we try to do things we haven't done before. Your readers need you to help them adopt a "can-do" attitude so they can approach learning with curiosity and confidence.

As you can see, developing training materials that work demands the same attention to your audience's situation, emotions, and interests that you bring to bear on other kinds of writing. It's a common mistake to consider training manuals, e-courses, tutorials, and other kinds of training materials as simple explanation. Keep in mind that many learners come to training materials feeling frustrated or intimated because they haven't been able to figure out how to do something on their own. Many adults, in particular, also bring to a learning experience a lifetime of negative learning experiences, sometimes going back to childhood. Consequently, creating learning materials that engage learners and stick with them requires you to think about not just how to inform your audience but also how to motivate them to pay attention to the information you have to share.

Before you start to develop your training materials, then, take some time to learn as much as you can about your learners, not just who they are but also the specific pieces of knowledge, beliefs, and attitudes they carry with them. Below you'll find few questions to guide you through that analysis so you can build your learning materials on the only solid ground available to you, the place where your audience is actually standing. You may find it helpful to complete the questions for various learner profiles (similar to the avatars for web writing you created in Chapter 4):

- What practical tasks do my learners want the training to help them perform?

- Why do they want to do those tasks?
- What knowledge about those tasks do my learners already have?
- What key pieces of knowledge or key skills are they missing?
- What related or similar kinds of tasks do the learners know how to do?
- What skills do they have that could form a foundation for skills they need to learn?
- How do my readers feel about learning the new task? What mental blocks might they be facing?

Principle 2: Map a Clear Learning Path (or Paths)

Analyzing your learners' previous knowledge, as well as their attitudes and beliefs, enables you to map out the territory you'll need to cover in order for them to master the knowledge and skills you're teaching. The next challenge is to guide them along a learning path that's easy for them to follow.

Our efficiency-loving brains thrive on structure, especially when it comes to learning new things. And they get pretty lazy about learning when there's no structure to guide the various phases of recognizing, storing, and retrieving new information. As you develop your training materials, structure your content to make it as effortless as possible for your reader to proceed through the learning process.[2]

Here are some organizational tips to help you help your learners:

- **Provide an overall description of the training.** Let learners know the major goals they'll achieve through the training, the topics the training will cover, and the format or method the learning will follow.
- **List specific learning outcomes.** Indicate the precise, practical takeaways learners will get from the training. An easy way to

---

[2]Julie Dirksen's book *Design for How People Learn*, 2nd ed., is chock-full of simple, straightforward advice for structuring learning materials to make them accessible and easy to remember (San Francisco, CA: New Riders, 2016).

express these is to start with the following prompt: *By the end of this training, you'll be able to...*

- **Create a picture of the learning journey.** As readers dive into your training materials, they'll be wondering how long the learning journey will take, what supplies they'll need to complete it, and how many stops there will be along the way. They'll also be looking for shortcuts and ways to bend the learning path to their individual needs and preferences.

  Depending on how diverse your anticipated audience is, you may want to provide multiple pathways through the training content. For instance, you might provide summaries of background modules so more experienced learners can skip over them. Or you might design content sections so learners can choose the order in which they read them.

- **Break content into small sections.** You might call these chapters, sections, modules, or steps. The label is irrelevant so long as you present the content in small, easy-to-digest bits that enable learners to feel they're making steady progress.

- **Use descriptive headings.** Make your headings specific, and make them sizzle so that they grab learner attention. Descriptive headings also play a key role in helping learners preview and review section content.

- **Summarize, summarize, summarize.** Forming those new neuronal pathways requires repetition, so recap key ideas in strategic places. Normally, those include the end of a section, transitions from one main idea to the next within a section, and the beginning of a new section.

Principle 3: Make Your Content Memorable

Our brains work nonstop processing a steady deluge of sensory and cognitive data, and only a small proportion of that gets stored in our short-term memory. An even slimmer proportion gets transferred to our long-term memory and "embedded" there. How do you improve the odds that your training content will win the lottery for long-term storage? You generate emotional resonance, invent mnemonics, and incorporate visuals.

1. Generate Emotional Resonance

When we associate strong emotions with incoming data, we're much more likely to embed that data in our long-term memory. You can generate emotional resonance by using feelings to frame your overall description of the training and your learning outcomes. What negative emotions does your audience feel now, without the knowledge and skills the training provides? What positive emotions will they feel once they've completed the training?

Stories also enable you to evoke strong emotions in your learners. Consider how you can weave stories into instruction and use scenarios for practice exercises.

2. Invent Mnemonics

Mnemonics are aids to memory, such as acronyms and rhymes. When we explored blogging in Chapter 6, you encountered an example of an acronym mnemonic, the PAVE method. The Finazz blog title I used as an example in that same chapter also created a mnemonic through rhyming: "Revenue is for vanity; profit is for sanity."

Besides helping learners recall information, mnemonics enable you to brand key learning concepts or processes, giving you an advantage in the market.

3. "Chunk" Information Items into Groups of Five or Fewer

The jury is currently out regarding the maximum number of items the human brain can keep in short-term memory. For decades, Miller's Law was thought to have decided the question. Research published by Harvard psychologist George Miller in 1956 found that the "magical number" for retention was "seven, plus or minus two."[3] However, more recent research has pointed out that a number of different variables affect the ability to recall discrete pieces of information and has proposed four as the new "magical number."[4]

---

[3]G. Miller. 1956. "The Magical Number Seven, Plus or Minus Two: Some Limits on Our Capacity for Processing Information," *Psychological Review* 63, no. 2, pp. 81–97.
[4]N. Cowan. 2000. "The Magical Number 4 in Short-term Memory: A Reconsideration of Mental Storage Capacity," *Behavioral and Brain Sciences* 24, pp. 87–185.

Insights from an Edutech Entrepreneur

Hussein Hallak is a serial entrepreneur whose latest product is CXO.ai, software that enables mentors to deliver curated content as e-mail courses personalized to the interests of their mentees. He also has an extensive training background, having taught marketing and entrepreneurship to a range of audiences, including members of Launch Academy, a tech incubator in Vancouver.

Hussein's experience as an edutech entrepreneur and a trainer has given him some great insights into how to break down complex concepts into teachable bits. Here are a few of those:

- **Read more.** "Writing, for me, is a combination of reading and writing," says Hussein. He reads widely, preferring books over web content because they "take a concept and break it down and go into it in depth."
- **Focus first.** When developing training, Hussein doesn't try to compress vast amounts of information into a single presentation or module. Instead, he zeroes in on what he calls "the core content" and builds from there. He recommends an organic approach: "Instead of thinking about what you want to say, think what you want to focus on, and the words will come."
- **Use groups of three.** Hussein stresses that learners need a clear structure in order to process and absorb information. He loves breaking things down into three elements. "I love the number three. It helps people understand that it's not an infinite thing that you need to do."

4. Incorporate Visuals

Regardless of our alleged "learning style" or "learning preference,"[5] of all the channels through which we receive information from the world around us, the visual channel produces the biggest impact on learning. The "pictorial superiority effect" ensures that "the more visual the input becomes, the more likely it is to be recognized—and recalled."[6]

Whether or not you believe your target audience to be "visual learners," incorporate elements of graphic design (such as text boxes, callouts, and icons) as well as visuals (such as charts, diagrams, infographics, line drawings, and photos) throughout your training materials.

Professionals who develop training materials call themselves "instructional designers," not "instructional writers," for good reason. When I consult with clients as an instructional designer, one of my chief tasks is to find creative ways to turn key teaching points into clear, compelling visuals. In many cases, the process of visualizing the content leads to a rethinking of the way that content is presented verbally. For example, let's say we want to convey a set of 10 best practices for safeguarding cybersecurity. In order for us to communicate that information visually and in a way that's simple to remember, the first step would be to narrow the list to three or four overarching best practices or themes, with each of those containing subpractices. With less than a handful of broad concepts to work with, we could then construct a visual "framework" (built of blocks or overlapping circles, perhaps) to help learners easily grasp and recall the content.

Figure 12.1 shows an example of a simple visual illustrating a set of learning concepts.

---

[5]While the notion of a preferred learning style has become popular in K-12 education, post-secondary education, and the corporate world, there's little empirical evidence to suggest that the concept holds any merit. Olga Khazan sums up some of the recent scholarly work making this point in her 2018 article for *The Atlantic*, "The Myth of 'Learning Styles'" (April 2018). https://getpocket.com/explore/item/the-myth-of-learning-styles, (accessed October 15, 2019).

[6]J. Medina. 2014. *Brain Rules: 12 Principles for Surviving and Thriving at Work, Home, and School*, 2nd ed. (Seattle, WA: Pear Press), "Vision," Kindle.

Five Principles for Creating Learning that "Sticks"

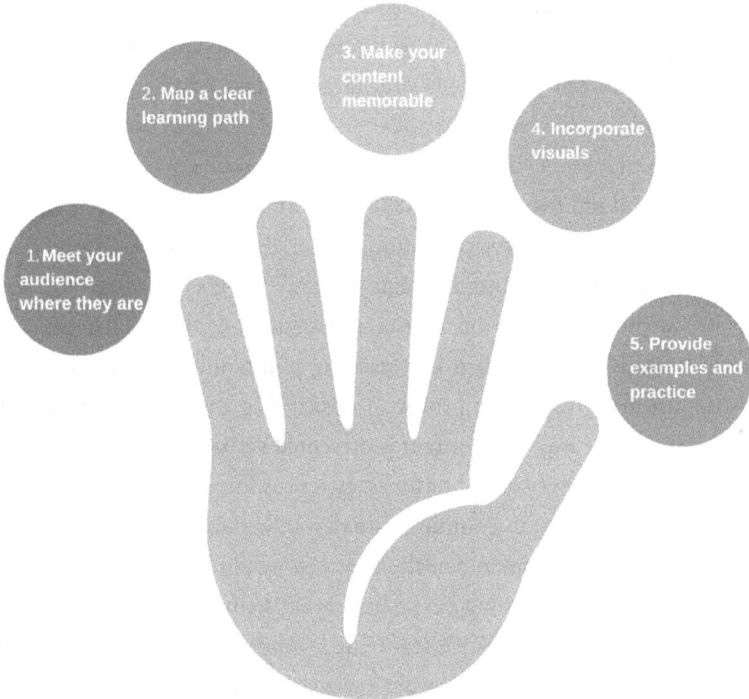

Follow this handful of simple guidelines to make your learning materials learner-centered, engaging, and impactful.

Figure 12.1 Example of a learning visual

Principle 4: Provide Examples and Practice

As noted earlier, many SMEs assume that learners will be able to "connect the dots" and link high-level concepts to real-world practice. If that were so, there'd be no need for you to develop training materials. You could simply rely on blog posts, journal articles, and white papers to develop the knowledge and skills your customers need.

Detailed, realistic examples and practice opportunities provide a bridge between the principles and ideas you're communicating and the real tasks learners need to do. You may find, in fact, that you spend as much time producing examples and practice exercises as you do creating your core content. If you're fortunate to be working with a team as you craft your training materials, you might consider engaging them in this part of the writing process.

As you develop practice exercises, consider ways to give learners feedback on their responses. Can you provide a model response, examples of different kinds of excellent responses, or an analysis of a typical response?

Principle 5: Create Tools for the Real World

The people reading your training materials are seeking practical information and skills they can use to achieve specific tasks. Well-designed training materials can take them only so far toward this goal. Ultimately, what they want and need are tools.

To complete your training content, provide user-friendly tools that make it easy for learners to apply what they've learned to their personal circumstances. Such tools might include worksheets, checklists, guidelines, pre-formatted spreadsheets, or short videos. Make these important training elements visually appealing, in compliance with your brand standards. Such tools also provide great opportunities to differentiate yourself in the market and to build up your brand identity.

Advice from a Neuroscientist-turned-trainer

Mandy Wintink has a PhD in psychology and neuroscience and teaches neuroscience classes at the University of Guelph. She also runs the Centre for Applied Neuroscience (CAN), based in Toronto. Through CAN, she teaches an integrated approach to life coaching that taps into her academic expertise as well as her training in yoga and meditation. Using this same holistic framework, she also delivers Brain Health and Wellness seminars for companies and public-sector organizations.

As Mandy moves among different learning audiences, she intentionally adapts. Practice, she says, makes it easier to flex your writing style as needed:

> I have to be really conscious of my words. I have to really step out of myself; it's changing my brain almost. I have to be very conscious of when I'm speaking in an academic voice and when I'm speaking in a general non-academic advice. I'm not talking the same way to every single person.

Mandy thinks of these different voices as different "hats" suitable to different situations. When she puts on her training hat (as opposed to her professor's hat), she chooses simple terms and keeps her sentences short, aiming to write at about a Grade 8 level. As someone with deep knowledge of her subject, she doesn't find this easy, but she's learned to focus on the essentials and leave out "all the icing on the cake that I want to provide."

Mandy also guards against offering too much theory and technical detail. "People say that they want to know neuroscience, but they don't," she explains. "They want to know a few things about the brain, but they don't actually want to know how the brain fully works because when I go into that, it's too deep for them, and they get lost."

As CAN evolves, Mandy continues to experiment with different approaches to delivering instruction. For instance, she started out by offering participants in her life coaching program a user manual but soon found that a "static document" didn't serve her learners well. Now, the program relies on a various of kinds of content, including videos and self-reflective exercises, to guide the learning experience. Such "multidimensional" content engages learners through different modalities, allows them to work at their own pace, and can be easily updated as the program continues to grow and change.

Checklist for Training Material

❏ Meets the audience where they are (not where you wish they were)

❏ Provides more practical information than theory and background

❏ Uses an empathetic, encouraging tone

❏ Maps a clear learning path by providing section overviews, headings, and summaries

❏ Makes content memorable:

- ○ Generates emotional resonance
- ○ Uses mnemonics
- ○ Chunks information items into groups of five or fewer
- ○ Incorporates visuals

❏ Includes tools for the real world

❏ Incorporates various kinds of content and, where possible, various forms of media

Parting Thoughts

Whether you've just finished reading this book cover to cover or have skimmed only a few chapters, now is the perfect time to take stock of what you've learned and consider what's next. I'd encourage you to spend a few minutes in personal reflection, thinking through these questions:

- **What's your biggest takeaway?**
- **What was the biggest surprise in what you learned?**
- **How will you apply what you've learned?** (Try to be as specific as you can so you create a goal to work toward.)
- **Do you need any help to apply what you've learned?** If so, where will you find it? Will you check out some of the resources mentioned in this book's notes? Enlist the support of a team member? Find yourself a writing buddy or mentor?
- **What other topics do you wish this book had covered?** What will you do to learn more about that subject?

As you think about other topics you wish we'd explored, please feel free to share them with me. You can reach me by e-mail at dawn@dawnhenwood.com. I'd love to hear your ideas for improving this book so it can help more people like you navigate the peculiar communication challenges that come with living the life of an innovative entrepreneur.

References

Canadian Radio-television and Telecommunications Commission. September 18, 2019. "Frequently Asked Questions about Canada's Anti-spam Legislation." https://crtc.gc.ca/eng/com500/faq500.htm.

CBC (based on a report by David Rémaillard). July 7, 2019. "Thousands of Desjardins Members Sign Petition Demanding New SINs," *CBC website*. https://www.cbc.ca/news/canada/montreal/desjardins-members-new-social-insurance-numbers-1.5202999.

Cialdini, R. 1993. *Influence: The Psychology of Persuasion*. New York, NY: William Morrow.

Covey, S. 2013. *The Seven Habits of Highly Effective People: Powerful Lessons in Personal Change*. 25th anniversary ed. New York, NY: Rosetta Books, Kindle.

Cowan, N. 2000. "The Magical Number 4 in Short-term Memory: A Reconsideration of Mental Storage Capacity." *Behavioral and Brain Sciences* 24, pp. 87–185.

Davidson, T. "How to Pitch Your Financial Projections," *Foresight website*. https://foresight.is/learn/presenting-financials, (accessed October 10, 2019).

Dirksen, J. 2016. *Design for How People Learn*. 2nd ed. San Francisco, CA: New Riders.

DocSend. n.d. "What We Learned from 200 Startups Who Raised $360M." https://docsend.com/view/p8jxsqr, (accessed October 10, 2019).

Dow, S., A. Glassco, J. Kass, M. Schwarz, D.L. Schwarz, and S.R. Klemmer. 2010. "Parallel Prototyping Leads to Better Design Results, more Divergence, and Increased Self-Efficacy." *ACM Transactions on Computer-Human Interaction* 17, no. 4, pp. 18, 1–24.

Duarte, N. 2014. *Slidedocs: Spread Ideas with Effective Visual Documents*. Santa Clara, CA: Duarte Inc.

Elbow, P. 2000. *Everyone Can Write*. New York, NY: Oxford University Press.

European Commission. n.d. "Rules for Businesses and Organisations." https://ec.europa.eu/info/law/law-topic/data-protection/reform/rules-business-and-organisations_en, (accessed September 21, 2019).

Federal Trade Commission. March. 2019. "CAN-SPAM Act: A Compliance Guide for Business." https://www.ftc.gov/tips-advice/business-center/guidance/can-spam-act-compliance-guide-business.

GlobalWebIndex. 2019. "Social: GlobalWebIndex's Flagship Report on the Latest Trends in Social Media," p. 3. https://www.globalwebindex.com/hubfs/Downloads/2019%20Q1%20Social%20Flagship%20Report.pdf?utm_campaign=Social%20report%20July%202019&utm_source=hs_automation&utm_medium=email&utm_content=74226065&_hsenc=p2ANqtz-8hAe1M2SewJ-ZkcZDE7ZiyEP2cyojPG9S-50l0_LT9PEH988ukfKXkrcGf3jz3vfAVdbX1mwwOE9w4olPKssky6pqXSg&_hsmi=74226065.

Godin, S. 2018. *This is Marketing.* New York, NY: Portfolio/Penguin, Kindle.

Gottschall, J. 2013. *The Storytelling Animal: How Stories Make Us Human.* New York, NY: Houghton Mifflin/Mariner Books, Kindle.

Heath, C., and D. Heath. 2013. *Decisive: How to Make Better Choices in Life and Work.* Toronto, Canada: Random House, Kindle.

Kafka, F. *The Metamorphosis.* Trans. D. Wyllie. Project Gutenberg. http://www.gutenberg.org/files/5200/5200-h/5200-h.htm, (accessed September 28, 2009).

Kress, G., and T. van Leeuwen. 1996. *Reading Images: The Grammar of Visual Design.* New York, NY: Routledge.

Lakoff, G. 2014. *The All New Don't Think of an Elephant!* White River Junction, VT: Chelsea Green Publishing, Kindle.

Medina, J. 2014. *Brain Rules: 12 Principles for Surviving and Thriving at Work, Home, and School.* 2nd ed. Seattle, WA: Pear Press, Kindle.

Miller, G. 1956. "The Magical Number Seven, Plus or Minus Two: Some Limits on Our Capacity for Processing Information." *Psychological Review* 63, no. 2, pp. 81–97.

Nielsen, J. April 16, 2006. "F-shaped Pattern for Reading Web Content (Original Study).". Nielsen Norman Group website, (accessed September 30, 2019). https://www.nngroup.com/articles/f-shaped-pattern-reading-web-content-discovered/.

Nielsen, J. "How Long Do Users Stay on Web Pages?" *Nielsen Norman Group website.* September 11, 2011. https://www.nngroup.com/articles/how-long-do-users-stay-on-web-pages/.

Norman, D. 2004. *Emotional Design: Why We Love (or Hate) Everyday Things.* New York, NY: Basic Books.

Pernice, K. August 4. 2019. "The Layer-cake Pattern of Scanning Content on the Web," *Nielsen Norman Group website.* https://www.nngroup.com/articles/layer-cake-pattern-scanning/, (accessed September 30, 2019).

Pipher, M. 2006. *Writing to Change the World.* New York, NY: Penguin, Kindle.

Porter, M. 1996. "What Is Strategy?" *Harvard Business Review* 74, no. 6, pp. 61–78.

Reddish, G. 2012. *Letting Go of the Words: Writing Web Content that Works.* 2nd ed. San Francisco, CA: Morgan Kaufmann.

Sharples, M. 1999. *How We Write: Writing as Creative Design.* London, UK: Routledge.

Silver, M. August 28, 2019. "Reducing Article Writing from 4 hours to 12 minutes," *Heart of Business blog.* https://www.heartofbusiness.com/2019/reducing-article-writing-from-4-hours-to-12-minutes/.

Skovholt, K., and J. Svennevig. 2013. "Responses and Non-responses in Workplace Emails." In *Handbook of the Pragmatics of Computer-Mediated Communication*, eds. by S. Herring and T. Virtanen. Berlin, Germany: Mouton de Gruyter, pp. 581–603. https://www.researchgate.net/publication/275958714_Skovholt_K_Svennevig_J_2013_Responses_and_Non-responses_in_Workplace_Emails_I_S_Herring_D_Stein_T_Virtanen_Eds_Handbook_of_the_Pragmatics_of_Computer-Mediated_Communication_Mouton_de_Gruyter_581-603.

Waltermire, K., and H. Perper. October 2019. "Improving Cybersecurity of Managed Service Providers: Supporting Small- and Medium-Size Businesses (draft)," *Website of the National Cybersecurity Center of Excellence.* https://www.nccoe.nist.gov/sites/default/files/library/project-descriptions/msp-ic-project-description-draft.pdf (accessed October 12, 2019.

Williams, J. 19891. "The Phenomenology of Error." *College Composition and Communication* 32, no. 2, pp. 152–168.

Wlodkowski, R.J. 2008. *Enhancing Adult Motivation to Learn.* 3rd ed. San Francisco, CA: Jossey-Bass.

About the Author

Dawn Henwood empowers innovators to communicate in clear, simple language that resonates with their target audience and produces results.

Dawn has a PhD in English from the University of Toronto and 20 years of experience as a writing consultant, instructor, and coach. Author of *A Writing Guide for IT Professionals* (Oxford University Press), she has created more than a dozen writing courses, including programs for one of the world's largest consulting firms and for Dalhousie University's College of Continuing Education.

Check out Dawn's website to access free resources, including her Weekly Writing Hack videos: www.dawnhenwood.com.

Index

OTHER TITLES IN OUR CORPORATE COMMUNICATION COLLECTION

Debbie DuFrene, Stephen F. Austin State University, *Editor*

- *Delivering Effective Virtual Presentations* by K. Virginia Hemby
- *New Insights into Prognostic Data Analytics in Corporate Communication* by Pragyan Rath and Kumari Shalini
- *Leadership Through A Screen: A Definitive Guide to Leading a Remote, Virtual Team* by Joseph Brady and Garry Prentice
- *Managerial Communication for Professional Development* by Reginald L. Bell and Jeanette S. Martin
- *Managerial Communication for Organizational Development* by Reginald L. Bell and Jeanette S. Martin
- *Business Report Guides: Routine and Nonroutine Reports and Policies, Procedures, and Instructions* by Dorinda Clippinger
- *Business Report Guides: Research Reports and Business Plans* by Dorinda Clippinger
- *Strategic Thinking and Writing* by Michael Edmondson
- *Conducting Business Across Borders: Effective Communication in English with Non-Native Speakers* by Adrian Wallwork
- *English Business Jargon and Slang: How to Use It and What It Really Means* by Suzan St. Maur
- *Business Research Reporting* by Dorinda Clippinger
- *64 Surefire Strategies for Being Understood When Communicating with Co-Workers* by Walter St. John
- *Communicating to Lead and Motivate* by William C. Sharbrough
- *Managerial Communication and the Brain: Applying Neuroscience to Leadership Practices* by Drik Remley

Announcing the Business Expert Press Digital Library

Concise e-books business students need for classroom and research

This book can also be purchased in an e-book collection by your library as

- *a one-time purchase,*
- *that is owned forever,*
- *allows for simultaneous readers,*
- *has no restrictions on printing, and*
- *can be downloaded as PDFs from within the library community.*

Our digital library collections are a great solution to beat the rising cost of textbooks. E-books can be loaded into their course management systems or onto students' e-book readers.
The **Business Expert Press** digital libraries are very affordable, with no obligation to buy in future years. For more information, please visit **www.businessexpertpress.com/librarians**. To set up a trial in the United States, please email **sales@businessexpertpress.com**.

www.ingramcontent.com/pod-product-compliance
Lightning Source LLC
Chambersburg PA
CBHW061213220326
41599CB00025B/4626